UNDERSTANDING BOAT DESIGN

UNDERSTANDING BOAT DESIGN

4th EDITION

Ted Brewer

International Marine
Camden, Maine

Published by International Marine

10 9 8 7 6 5 4

Library of Congress Cataloging-in-Publication Data
Brewer, Edward S.
    Understanding boat design / Ted Brewer.--4th ed.
       p.   cm.
    Includes bibliographic references and index.
    ISBN 0-87742-392-X (acid-free paper)
    1. Boats and boating--Design and construction. I. Title.
VM321.B77   1994
623.8'223--dc20   93-28302
                          CIP

Questions regarding the content of this book should be addressed to:
        International Marine
        P.O. Box 220
        Camden, ME 04843

Questions regarding the ordering of this book should be addressed to:
        The McGraw-Hill Companies
        Customer Service Department
        P.O. Box 547
        Blacklick, OH 43004
        Retail customers: 1-800-822-8158
        Bookstores: 1-800-722-4726

 *Understanding Boat Design* is printed on recycled paper containing a minimum of 50% total recycled fiber with 10% postconsumer de-inked fiber.

Printed by R. R. Donnelley, Crawfordsville, IN

Design by Patrice M. Rossi

Production by Molly Mulhern

Edited by Jon Eaton, Fritz Burke, Tom McCarthy

To my wife, Betty,
who loves boats
as much as I do.

Contents

Preface   ix

CHAPTER

1. **Boats for Every Purpose**   *1*
2. **Hull Shapes**   *9*
3. **Interpreting the Lines Drawing**   *21*
4. **Lateral Plane**   *38*
5. **Sailboat Rigs**   *49*
6. **Powering**   *58*
7. **Aesthetics**   *62*
8. **The Accommodation Layout**   *70*
9. **Safety at Sea**   *78*
10. **Construction**   *81*
11. **Plans, The Designer, and You**   *96*
12. **Amateur Boatbuilding**   *102*

APPENDICES

A Portfolio of Brewer Designs   *105*
United States Coast Guard Auxiliary Courtesy Examination   *128*
Suggested Reading   *134*
A Short Glossary   *136*

Index   *144*

Preface

Understanding Boat Design was born over 25 years ago when Jim Betts and I were setting up the correspondence school called Yacht Design Institute. We needed a general overview of small craft design to acquaint the students with the terminology of the profession and to teach them the rudiments of hull shape, vessel types, rigs, and construction. Since no such book was available, I buckled down to write what became the first edition of this book. It was, indeed, a labor of love, as yacht design has been my life and I have always enjoyed teaching others. Eventually we had the book published privately, but we distributed it only to those taking the design course.

It was a great aid to our students, and when Bob Wallstrom bought out Jim's interest in the school in 1970, he saw that the little volume could be useful to a broader audience of sailors and powerboaters as well. Bob approached International Marine, and they expressed immediate interest and took over the publishing and sales of *Understanding Boat Design*,

including selling the books to us for our students!

The 64-page, staple-binding book went through several printings, but, as happens to all books on technical subjects, it grew dated over the years, missing more and more of the new innovations that continually crop up in small craft design. This new volume has been greatly expanded and almost completely rewritten, and it contains information on many aspects of design that were not even thought of back in 1968.

I hope you will find *Understanding Boat Design* readable and enjoyable, but more important, I hope you will learn something about small craft design, both power and sail, that you did not know before. If you do, then the book has fulfilled my purpose in writing it.

Ted Brewer
Lyman, Washington
September 1993

CHAPTER ONE

Boats for Every Purpose

E very year thousands of people attend boat shows, visit dealers, and talk to yacht brokers in the search of the perfect boat; perfect for them, that is. Unfortunately there is no such thing as a perfect boat, no single design that does everything well. Every boat is a compromise of virtues whether it is an outboard fishing boat or a multimillion dollar megayacht.

In many ways, buying a boat is like buying a car. You weigh your needs and desires against your bank balance (they rarely match) and head for "gasoline alley." There you look over the usual lineup of prosaic sedans, roomy vans, flashy sports cars, and rugged four-wheel drives—an endless assortment of makes, models, styles, colors, sizes, and options. Boats are also available in bewildering varieties of sail, power, racer, cruiser, fisherman, ski boat, houseboat, inboard, outboard, fiberglass, wood, metal—you name it.

Still, regardless of type, every boat is a compromise of four basic factors: seaworthiness, comfort, performance, and cost. Let's consider these one at a time.

Obviously it is unfair to compare the seaworthiness of a family daysailer with that of an ocean racer, and an outboard fishing boat does not need the seagoing ability of a bluewater motoryacht. However, all boats must meet a certain level of seaworthiness to suit their particular purpose, and they can and should be compared with others of their type. For example, if you are considering two outboard fishing boats, you might find that one has much less freeboard than the other. This would make it less able to take rough water in its stride, and would limit its use to protected waters and rivers. It would not be a suitable boat for salmon fishing in the challenging waters of the Northwest, but it might be the better boat if you need it for bass fishing in small and quiet lakes. Seaworthiness also includes structural quality to a large extent. The boat that is better built of higher quality materials will be longer lived, stronger, and more seaworthy than an identical sister built to a lower standard and a lower price.

Performance is also relative. An ocean racer is faster than a daysailer, but if we compare two daysailers we may find that one is beamier, heavier, and spreads considerably less sail area than the other. Obviously it will be the slower boat. On the other hand, the faster boat may be too exciting to sail on leisurely family outings; the slower boat could well be the best choice if that is its main purpose in life.

Comfort is determined to a large extent by size. As a rule a larger boat is more comfortable in heavy weather, unless it is a stripped-out racing machine. Comfort also depends, to a degree, upon weight. A heavier boat has an easier motion in a seaway, and it can carry greater amounts of fuel, water, and stores that add comfort on a long voyage. However, added weight may adversely affect performance.

The fourth and final factor in the great boat compromise is cost—in crass terms, money. The less you care about cost, the more of the other qualities you can obtain. When cost is no object, a boat can be faster, more seaworthy, stronger, and more comfortable than a similar-sized vessel built inexpensively for the broad market appeal. For that matter, the boat can be bigger. Cost also includes the expense of operating a vessel; a twin-screw gas guzzler has higher operating costs than a slower boat powered by a single engine of modest power. Maintenance costs, which are usually influenced by size, must also be considered. Some of these are marine berthing, winter haulouts, and bottom painting.

The following chart shows how a few different boats might line up.

Factor	Seaworthiness	Comfort	Performance	Cost
SAIL				
America's Cup racer	5%	1%	92%	2%
IOR Racer	25%	10%	60%	5%
Ocean cruiser	30%	30%	20%	20%
Coastal cruiser	25%	25%	25%	25%
Weekender	20%	20%	25%	35%
Daysailer	15%	15%	30%	40%
POWER				
Ocean racer	20%	5%	65%	10%
Ocean cruiser	30%	30%	20%	20%
Express cruiser	15%	30%	30%	25%
Houseboat	5%	40%	15%	40%
Sports fisherman	25%	25%	30%	20%

Not every boat will match the percentages of its type, of course, but rarely will a gain in one factor be made without some sacrifice in another. An express cruiser, for example, might jump from 30% to 35% in the performance factor if bigger engines are fitted, but then the cost factor drops from 25% to 20% because the boat now costs more to buy and to operate.

It is important that buyers be realistic in evaluating their needs. Too often a family with a two-week annual vacation dreams of long ocean voyages to romantic ports. With this in mind, they buy a heavy, bluewater cruiser that never gets out of sight of land due to their limited leisure time. Later they find that it is slow, expensive, and costly to maintain, and they realize they would be happier with a sprightlier coastal cruiser. Similarly, the skipper interested in gunkholing and relaxed cruising will be unhappy with a deep-draft, skinned-out racing machine. The yachtsman who has the desire, time, and finances for ocean racing wants a yacht with the accent on speed and seaworthiness.

The powerboat owner must also consider fuel costs. The price of gas and diesel fuel is rising steadily; it is well to remember the little adage that was in the front of the MG car owner's handbook over 40 years ago: "Speed costs money." Consider two boats, one a fast express cruiser and the other a slower displacement boat. The first might use a gallon of gas for every mile it travels, and if it is run at 15 knots for six hours it will use 90 gallons, about $125 worth of fuel at today's prices. The slower vessel, cruising at 8 knots and getting 3 miles per gallon, uses about $22 worth of fuel in the same day. You sure won't travel as far in the slower boat, but you will have the same happy hours afloat, the scenery will pass by slowly enough to be savored, and the lower fuel cost may allow you to travel twice as far in the long run.

Obviously, if you are looking for a boat, it pays to review your requirements carefully, consider your available time, weigh your desires against your needs, and balance it all against your ability to pay. If you are inexperienced, read all you can about the boats that interest you, talk to other owners, and perhaps take one of the fine U.S. Power Squadron courses in boat handling and safety. It will stand you in good stead when you do get your dream ship.

The Language of the Naval Architect

Before we can go into the faults and virtues of the various hull forms, you need to be familiar with a few terms. The following characteristics are common to all boats, and their measurements should be available from the designer or builder if you are contemplating a specific vessel.

Length Overall (abbreviated *LOA*)—The length of the yacht excluding bowsprits and boomkins (see Figure 1-1). It is a common term but can be misused. Length on Deck is a better way to describe a boat's size as it eliminates overhanging rails, clipper bows, and other features that do not add to interior space.

Load Waterline Length (*LWL*)—The length of the yacht on its flotation lines. If the designer calculated correctly, this is the same as the Design Waterline (DWL) when the boat is new. Most boats, however,

sink a bit or change trim over the years as they accumulate gear, provisions, and cultch, so the actual LWL is rarely what was drawn on the plans.

Beam—The greatest width of the vessel, often written as Beam (Max).

Beam WL—The greatest width at the LWL.

Displacement—The weight of water that the boat displaces. This is equal to the boat's weight. Displacement is usually expressed in pounds in small craft but may also be given in cubic feet. Multiply the cubic feet by 64 to get the displacement in pounds. Large yachts may have the displacement given in tons, but bear in mind that these are long tons of 2240 pounds and each ton contains 35 cubic feet of sea water.

Center of Buoyancy (*CB*)—The location of the center of the boat's displacement. It is obvious that the CB is located below the LWL, but it is usually calculated only in a fore-and-aft direction. It is expressed as a distance from the bow, or perhaps from amidships, or as a percentage of the boat's waterline length. The CB is the center of the water's support and also the center of the vessel's weight, or Center of Gravity (CG). For example, if you walk forward on your boat from amidships to the bow you move the CG ahead slightly. The boat sinks by the bow as you move, changing the underwater shape and shifting the CB forward so that it is always in line with the changing CG (Figure 1-2).

Center of Flotation (*CF*)—The center of the area of the load waterline. It is the location about which the vessel changes trim as weights are moved, like the center of a teeter-totter.

Pounds Per Inch Immersion (*PPI*)—The weight required to sink the vessel 1 inch in the water.

Moment to Trim 1 Inch (*MT1*)—The moment, expressed in foot-pounds, that moves the bow up

FIGURE 1-1

The language of the naval architect.

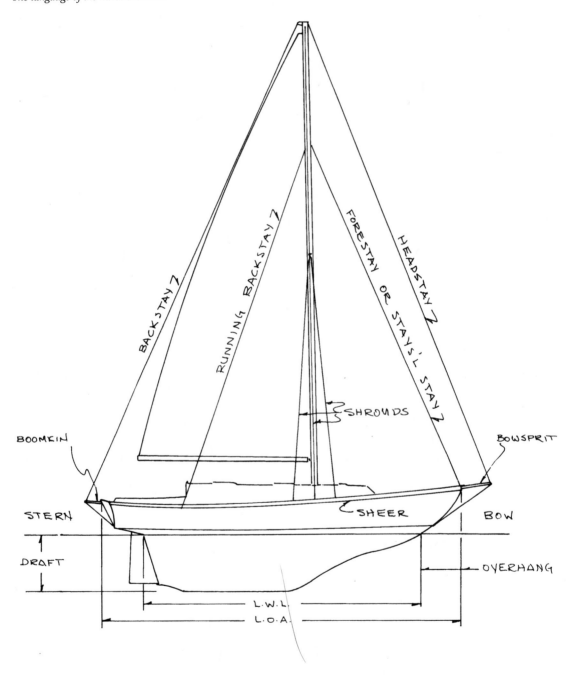

FIGURE 1-2
Center of Buoyancy and Center of Gravity simplified.

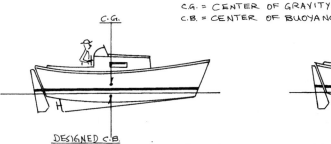

C.G. = CENTER OF GRAVITY
C.B. = CENTER OF BUOYANCY

DESIGNED C.B.
THE BOAT IS IN PERFECT TRIM WHEN THE CENTER OF GRAVITY IS ABOVE THE DESIGNED CENTER OF BUOYANCY.

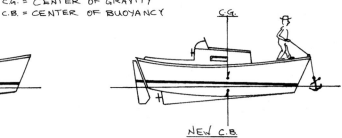

NEW C.B.
WHEN A WEIGHT IS MOVED, OR ADDED, THE C.G. MOVES ACCORDINGLY. THE BOAT THEN CHANGES TRIM UNTIL THE NEW C.B. IS IN LINE WITH THE C.G.

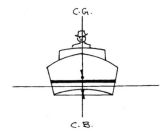

SIMILARLY, THE BOAT WILL HEEL IF WEIGHT IS MOVED OR ADDED OFF THE CENTER LINE.

and the stern down (or vice versa) a total of 1 inch. For example, if a vessel has a MTI of 900 foot-pounds, a 150-pound man moving 6 feet forward puts the bow down and the stern up a total of 1 inch. Because the boat changes trim around its CF, and that point is usually abaft amidships, the bow moves more than the stern. In our hypothetical case the bow might sink ¾ inch and the stern rise ¼ inch to make up the total trim change of 1 inch.

Wetted Surface (WS)—The underwater area of the hull, including rudder and centerboard, usually expressed in square feet. A boat with a high WS has more skin friction and is slower in light air than a boat of equal size and sail area with a low WS. For this reason, most modern sailing yachts sport fin keels and spade rudders, as these offer less WS than the older full-keel designs. The figure has little significance for powerboats.

Prismatic Coefficient (Cp)—A nondimensional figure used for comparison of hull shapes. It is derived from the displacement in cubic feet divided by the square feet of the amidships area times the LWL:

$$\frac{\text{Displacement}}{\text{Amidships Area x LWL}}$$

To simplify, if you took a block of wood the length

FIGURE 1-3
Prismatic coefficient.

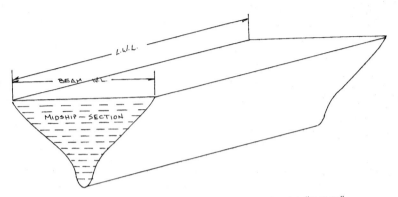

THE PRISMATIC COEFFICIENT IS THE AMOUNT OF THIS "PRISM"
THAT REMAINS AFTER THE HULL IS CARVED OUT.

of the LWL and shaped to the underwater portion of the midship section, then carved it away to model the ends of the boat, the Cp is the remaining percentage of the original midship-shaped block (Figure 1-3).

The proper Cp for a boat depends on its intended speed/length ratio (the speed in knots divided by the square root of the LWL). The Cp can range widely, from .48 or so for a sailboat intended for light air use up to .80 or more for a planing motorboat. The following table shows the correct Cps for various speed/length ratios.

Powerboat hulls want Cps matched to their intended operating speeds—say, .60 to .62 for a displacement powerboat, .66 to .70 and higher for a semidisplacement (or semiplaning—it's the same thing!) hull. Sailboats generally have average speed/length ratios of about 1.1 and Cps in the .54–.55 range. It is best if the Cp is a bit on the high side, because the added resistance from having too high a Cp for low-speed work is less serious than the resistance from having too low a Cp at higher speeds.

Center of Lateral Plane (*CLP*)—The center of the underwater area of the hull. Important only for

Speed/Length Ratio	Prismatic Coefficient
1.0 and below	.525
1.1	.54
1.2	.58
1.3	.62
1.4	.64
1.5	.66
1.6	.68
1.7	.69
1.8 and above	.70

sailboats because it is a guide to the location of the sails and rig.

Center of Effort (*CE*)—The center of the sail area. It is usually calculated using 100% of the *foretriangle area* (the area bounded by the headstays, the mast,

FIGURE 1-4

Parts of a boat.

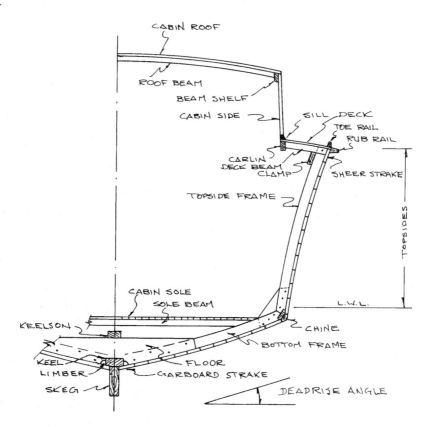

and the foredeck). The CE must be ahead of the CLP in order to avoid a heavy *weather helm*. We'll look at weather helm and *helm balance* in Chapter 5.

Deadrise Angle—The angle the bottom of the boat makes with the LWL when viewed from the ends (Figure 1-4). A flat-bottom boat has zero deadrise, while a deeply veed hull has great deadrise. Powerboats that have a lot of deadrise forward and less deadrise at the transom are called *warped bottom* hulls. Those that carry the same deadrise angle from bow to stern are called *monohedron* hulls.

Topsides—To many people this means the deck and cabin, but they are wrong. The topsides is the part of the hull below the *sheer line* (deck edge) and above the LWL.

Displacement/Length Ratio—A nondimensional figure obtained by dividing the displacement in long tons (long ton = 2240 pounds) by .01 LWL cubed, or $Dt/(.01\ LWL)^3$. This figure allows us to compare the displacement of hulls of different sizes. The lower the D/L ratio, the smaller the waves generated by the hull as it passes through the water, and the smaller the wavemaking resistance.

Generally, for sailboats, ratios under 100 are considered to be ultralight, 100 to 200 is light, 200 to 300 is moderate, 300 to 400 is heavy, and over 400 is ultraheavy by today's standards. Most cruising sailboats fall into the moderate range. Powerboats may vary between planing hulls with ratios below 170 or so and semiplaning hulls in the 180 to 250 range.

Sail Area/Displacement Ratio—The sail area in square feet divided by the displacement in cubic feet to the 2/3 power, or SA/Dcf $^{.667}$. Ratios much below 15 indicate a lightly canvassed boat and are suited to motorsailers. Offshore cruisers have ratios in the 15 to 16 range, coastal cruisers 16 to 17. Ocean racers may fall in the 17 to 20 range, while ratios over 20 are usually given only to daysailers, class racers, and other high-performance boats.

Speed/Length Ratio—We ran into this term in the discussion of prismatic coefficients. It is given by the formula $V/\sqrt{L}$. For example, a 400-foot LWL ship traveling at 20 knots has a speed/length ratio of 1.0, as does a 36-foot LWL sailboat moving at a leisurely 6 knots. On the other hand, a 40-foot LWL motorboat moving at 20 knots has a S/L ratio of 3.16.

All boats can be divided into three general categories depending upon their maximum S/L ratios. Displacement hulls obtain no lift from their speed. Their maximum S/L ratio is 1.34. After that, despite added power, they just dig the stern in and go little, if any, faster. Typical displacement boats are ocean liners, tugs, trawlers, sailboats, canoes, and rowboats.

The semidisplacement (or semiplaning) hull is usually characterized by round bilges and a transom wide enough to provide some lift from the water flow beneath the hull. Such a boat is capable of high speeds, and has a maximum S/L ratio of 1.5 or so up to 2.5. Examples are Maine lobsterboats, some lightweight, fast dinghies and daysailers, and many older power cruisers.

The planing hull runs at S/L ratios of over 2.5 up to 10 or more (let me off!). These boats have hard chines and wide transoms to provide the needed lift so they can get "over the hump" and plane on top of the water. Typical planing hulls are the modern runabouts, sportfishing boats, and express cruisers. A very few ultralight and super-stable sailboats can achieve planing speeds on occasion, given a good breeze and a flat sea.

Comfort Ratio—I dreamed this one up, tongue in cheek, for a magazine article some years ago. However, it is now accepted by many as a measure of the motion comfort of a boat and, between boats of similar size and type, can provide a reasonable guide. It is based on the fact that the quickness of motion or corkiness of a hull in a choppy sea is what causes discomfort and seasickness. That corkiness is determined by two main factors: the beam of the hull and the area of the waterline. The formula is as follows:

$$\frac{\text{Displacement}}{65 \times (.7\text{LWL}+.3\text{LOA}) \times B^{1.333}}$$

where Displacement is measured in pounds and LWL and LOA are measured in feet. Lightweight boats and smaller yachts that have a higher beam/length ratio will rate poorly on the comfort scale while, as we would expect, heavy oceangoing cruisers rate more favorably. The ratio ranges from 10 or less for a lightweight day cruiser up to the higher 50s or 60s for a husky double-ender such as the old Colin Archer sailing pilot boats. Average ocean cruisers come up somewhere in the mid-30s.

CHAPTER TWO

Hull Shapes

T he best way to begin a study of hull shapes is by examining *midship sections*. The midship section of a boat is a slice taken athwartship right through the hull, halfway between the bow and stern. The shape of the midship section tells us the basic form of the hull—flat bottom, V bottom, or round bottom. A study of the midship section shape can tell us much more, though, such as whether the boat is tender or stable, hard riding or with an easy motion, even fast or slow. Let's start with the flat-bottom hull.

The Flat-Bottom Hull

The flat-bottom boat is an ideal type for the beginning amateur builder because it is the simplest to build, goes together quickly, and requires fewer tools and usually less money than more complex shapes. Flat-bottom boats have a deserved reputation for pounding in head seas, but intelligent design can reduce this substantially provided the vessel is used as intended.

The box scow (Figure 2-1A), the simplest form, is rectangular with sloping ends. Its use is limited to children's tiny play-boats and huge garbage scows. It

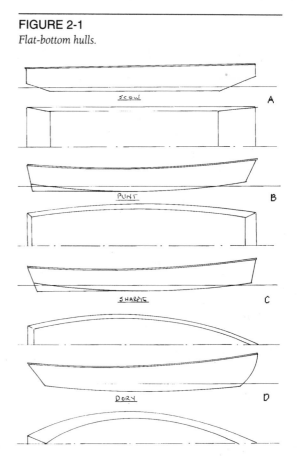

FIGURE 2-1
Flat-bottom hulls.

SCOW   A

PUNT   B

SHARPIE   C

DORY   D

has little to recommend it except utter simplicity. A more advanced scow shape (Figure 2-1B) shows a rockered bottom and, usually, some flare and curvature to the sides. Due to its simplicity, roominess, and shoal draft this form can still be used to advantage in protected waters. New Jersey garveys and Maine sloops built along these lines in sizes of 45 feet and more were used in coastal waters for fishing and cargo carrying. The scow would still make an interesting and inexpensive sailing or houseboat cruiser, but it pounds in a chop and is not at home in open waters when powered to higher speeds.

The sharpie form (Figure 2-1C) was developed in the 1800s in Connecticut for use in the Long Island oyster industry, but the design spread rapidly to the Chesapeake, Florida, the Great Lakes, and the West Coast due to its reputation for seaworthiness, its ease of construction, and its ability to sail on a heavy dew. Large sharpies were used as mailboats, and even as gunboats off the coast of Africa. The form is characterized by narrow beam—about one fourth the length—and a pointed bow. Many sharpies were built as double-enders (pointed at both ends). The topsides were generally well flared to increase reserve stability and dryness.

The sharpie is a fast sailer when reaching in a good breeze but should be sailed upright and not allowed to heel excessively. Thus they tend to pound when driven to windward in a chop. The sharpie is best suited to coastal cruising in waters where shelter is reasonably close at hand, but an experienced skipper can make the occasional long passage if he is careful to pick his weather.

The sailing sharpie's big drawback is a long centerboard trunk that splits the cabin in two and divides the accommodations. Some designs feature twin centerboards, bilge boards, or leeboards to leave the cabin clear. Another disadvantage is the lack of headroom. High freeboard and cabins are dangerous in a narrow and shallow hull because they add

weight and windage, adversely affecting stability. This makes it difficult to safely obtain standing headroom in a true sharpie under 40 feet.

The sharpie can make an able powerboat if the design incorporates a deep forefoot to reduce pounding. The bow should have a sharp entrance so the hull slices through the seas rather than rising on one wave and slapping down on the next. Such a boat should be limited to semidisplacement speeds; this permits a narrower stern with better low-speed performance when slowed by heavy weather. The sharpie should also be fitted with a deep skeg to give the hull some bite on the water and reduce yawing in steep following seas.

Dory hulls (Figure 2-1D) are beamier than the sharpie for their length, have more rocker, a narrower bottom, much more flare to the topsides, and typically, a very narrow or pointed bottom aft leading up to a tombstone-shaped transom. The boat is initially very tender due to the narrow bottom, so small dories will heel alarmingly at the slightest shift of crew weight. However, the flared topsides provide great reserve stability and have given the Banks dory an enviable reputation for seaworthiness. An outside keel with heavy ballast is mandatory for a sailing cruiser. Many designs based on a dory hull show a widening of the stern to provide increased initial stability.

The sailing dory operates at greater heel angles than other flat-bottom boats due to her narrower bottom, and so has less tendency to pound because she presents her chine to the seas rather than her flat bottom. Though slower than a sharpie, a cruising dory with outside ballast can be made self-righting from a severe knockdown. Thus she is suitable for longer offshore passages, although still not the ideal vessel for ocean voyages.

Dories make able low-speed powerboats and can be driven economically with small engines. Like the sharpie, weights should be kept low and high cabin houses avoided to maintain maximum stability. Such

FIGURE 2-2
A 27-foot dory cruiser.

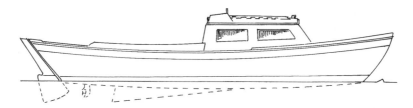

a boat takes heavy weather in stride and comes up smiling. Figure 2-2 shows a 27-foot dory cruiser powered by an 18-hp outboard in a motorwell. The boat was regularly used for weekend cruising and sportfishing off the coast of Maine. She cruised along at an easy 6 knots and proved inexpensive to build and operate.

To reach planing speeds, the dory hull is modified with a wide transom and reduced rocker aft. Because of the heavily flared topsides and longer bow over-hang, the boat is less prone to pounding than a sharpie but still not suited to offshore use. The wide transom does increase stability but also reduces low-speed efficiency, so the best compromise might be to limit modified dories to semidisplacement speeds and widen the transom only enough to prevent excessive squatting at a moderate speed/length ratio.

In general, the points to look for in all flat-bottom boats are modest freeboard and upperworks in order to reduce windage and weight aloft and maintain maximum stability. Sailboats should not have excessive keel rocker, as it is detrimental to speed. A fine entrance is desirable for both sail and power, while a fairly deep forefoot in powerboats reduces the tendency to pound in a chop. Well-flared topsides are a must to prevent spray from being blown back over the boat every time the bow hits a wave, and to add to reserve buoyancy and stability. Powerboats should have a good-sized skeg to aid in steering and provide

directional stability. While a skeg is often eliminated on small trailerable cruisers, remember that the boat is intended to operate in the water, not on a trailer. It seems foolish to compromise seaworthiness for trailering ease.

The Arc-Bottom Hull

The arc bottom (Figure 2-3) is obtained by curving a flat bottom athwartship to increase displacement without a great increase in wetted area. It is limited to sailing craft and is not popular due to the increased difficulty of construction.

The V-Bottom or Deadrise Hull

V-bottom hulls come in a wider variety of shapes and types than flat-bottom hulls and are more difficult to catalog. Many designs fall between the types we will describe. You will have to form your own opinion of their virtues based on knowledge and experience.

The modified sharpie hull (Figure 2-4A) has increasing deadrise from bow to stern and is commonly seen on many daysailers and small cruising sailboats. Low-speed motorboats could also use this form to produce an economical, easily driven vessel.

FIGURE 2-3

The arc-bottom hull.

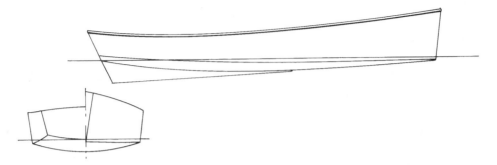

The Rosslyn model sharpie (Figure 2-4B), developed on Long Island in the late 1800s, had a flat bottom amidships with deadrise increasing both forward and aft. Both types are attempts to increase displacement, reduce wetted surface, and provide a better prismatic coefficient to increase performance. The Rosslyn model would also lend itself to a low-speed power-boat, and the shape is quite similar to some husky, Japanese offshore fishing vessels.

Scows also have been built with hulls similar to the Rosslyn model, flat amidships with deadrise increasing toward the bow and stern (Figure 2-4C). Good-sized schooners (40 feet LOA x 12 feet beam) were built along these lines and were popular in the late 1800s on the Gulf of Mexico, where they were used as cargo carriers and fishing boats. They were reported to sail well, and would make interesting sailing houseboats today. The sailing dory can also be modified, with deadrise commencing amidships and increasing to the stern, which is usually fitted with a wider transom. This alteration increases initial stability and improves the sailing qualities of the dory hull.

The V-bottom yacht hull (Figure 2-4D) shows increased deadrise and more keel rocker than the modified sharpies. Such boats can make very seaworthy cruisers, and many sailboats of this hull form have circumnavigated the globe. Steep deadrise and

great keel rocker increase displacement, allowing powerboats to carry heavy cargo, and sailboats, heavy outside ballast. These features also tend to reduce pounding, but the added displacement may have a detrimental effect on performance if the deadrise and rocker are carried to excess.

Many V-bottom sailboats and a few low-speed powerboats (tugs, trawlers) have been designed with two or more chines. This enables the designer to approximate the shape and characteristics of a round-bilge hull and obtain better performance by reducing turbulence and wetted surface (Figure 2-5). The extra chines add to the labor of building but can be very worthwhile if top performance is desired and the builder hesitates to tackle a round-bilge craft. The chines add little extra material cost and often add to resale value.

When we speak of V-bottom boats, most people think of a high-speed motorboat. The characteristics of such a hull (Figure 2-6) are a fairly high chine line forward that submerges just forward of midships and continues aft almost parallel to the LWL. The stern is wide to enable the vessel to get up onto a plane, and there is little rocker to the chine or keel abaft amidships. The hull deadrise is quite steep forward and reduces toward the stern; such hulls are often referred to as modified V-bottom, varying-deadrise, or

FIGURE 2-4
V-bottom hulls.

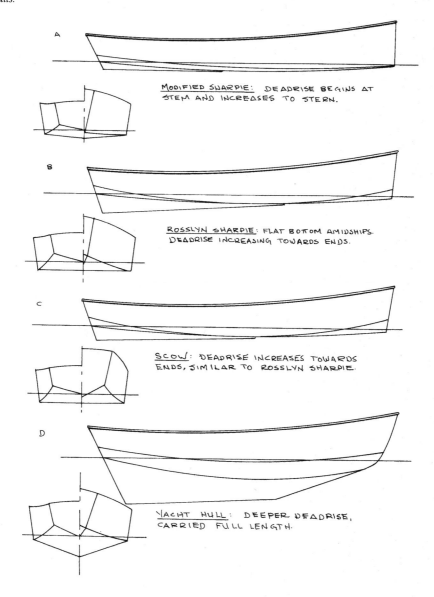

A

MODIFIED SHARPIE: DEADRISE BEGINS AT
STEM AND INCREASES TO STERN.

B

ROSSLYN SHARPIE: FLAT BOTTOM AMIDSHIPS.
DEADRISE INCREASING TOWARDS ENDS.

C

SCOW: DEADRISE INCREASES TOWARDS
ENDS, SIMILAR TO ROSSLYN SHARPIE.

D

YACHT HULL: DEEPER DEADRISE,
CARRIED FULL LENGTH.

warped-bottom. For example, the Deer Isle 28 lines shown in Figure 3-2 have a deadrise angle of about 35 degrees forward, 15 degrees amidships, and 9 degrees aft. One fault of some designs is that the chine is too low forward and enters the water too close to the bow. This may be an attempt to increase interior space in the bow, but such boats tend to pound heavily and push a wall of water ahead of them at low speeds

HULL SHAPES

FIGURE 2-5
The Murray 33 shows how a double chine hull can closely approach the shape of a round bilge vessel.

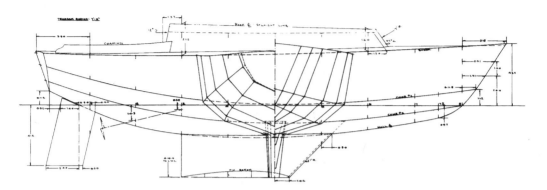

because the forward sections have too little deadrise.

The hull sections forward should be convex rather than flat or concave (Figure 2-7). A convex section is best because it mushes into head seas with a gentle deceleration rather than thumping down heavily. An angle of about 25 degrees from horizontal is desirable for hull sections that clear the water on a wave; this angle substantially reduces pounding when the boat comes back down. Another argument in favor of convex sections is that they are stronger than concave and better able to resist the terrific beating that a planing hull takes when moving at high speeds in a seaway. Since solid water can ride up the sections because there is no reverse angle to throw it off, a spray rail is needed. If no spray rail is fitted, or built into the mold of a fiberglass hull, the boat will be wet.

Deep-V powerboat hulls, pioneered by Raymond Hunt, carry their deadrise all the way to the stern rather than having the deadrise diminish abaft midships (Figure 2-8). The boats are noted for soft riding in choppy seas and have proved very able. Although the ultimate speed potential of a deep-V hull is not as great as the old warped-bottom style in calm waters, their ability to maintain high speed in a seaway makes up for it. The type is *de rigueur* for offshore racing.

FIGURE 2-6
Warped-bottom V planing hull.

FIGURE 2-7
Planing hull bottom sections.

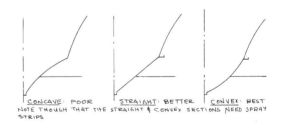

FIGURE 2-8
Deep-V planing hull.

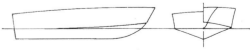

The deep-V hull is not as stable as the warped-bottom, particularly at rest; thus the latter shape is often advantageous for the average small cruiser, which is rarely pushed to top speed in heavy seas.

Smaller deep-V hulls rarely have a skeg fitted, since their deeper keel line contributes to course keeping. Larger boats may have a skeg fitted to protect propellers and rudders. Warped-bottom planing hulls need a skeg because the wide, flattish stern can yaw in following seas at lower speeds and contribute to difficult steering, with the danger of broaching and possible capsize in heavy weather.

Many amateur builders select V-bottom designs with an eye to simplifying construction by using sheet-plywood planking. This can be a serious error unless the boat was designed for plywood construction. Only boats all of whose hull sections are relatively parallel, or boats designed by the conical method of projection, can be sheet-plywood planked (Figure 2-9). The latter designs show definite convex rounding of the sections where the angles change rapidly between hull stations. If the sections are neither parallel nor convex, it is wise to check with the designer before assuming that sheet plywood can be used for planking.

FIGURE 2-9

Non-parallel sections are not suited to sheet plywood planking.

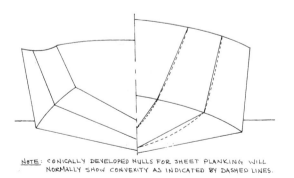

NOTE: CONICALLY DEVELOPED HULLS FOR SHEET PLANKING WILL NORMALLY SHOW CONVEXITY AS INDICATED BY DASHED LINES.

The Round-Bottom Hull

Round-bottom (perhaps round-bilge is a better word) hulls fall into three categories. The U section (Figure 2-10A) is used in dinghies, daysailers, and light to moderate-displacement cruising and racing sailboats of all sizes. Semidisplacement powerboats, and a few planing types, also use a modified U section.

In general, the round-bilge hull is superior to the flats or V-bottom hull for offshore and rough-water usage. It is stronger and has a slower roll with less snap than a chine hull of the same general size. For sailing yachts or semidisplacement powerboats, the shape reduces wetted surface and eliminates turbulence along the chines, cutting drag and increasing performance. Small daysailers and cruisers may have centerboards, but the larger cruisers are more often fitted with fin keels and either spade or skeg-hung rudders. Modern, fast cruisers and racers have little fore-and-aft rocker, flattish sections athwartship, and wide sterns to increase the prismatic coefficient and permit higher speeds in a strong breeze.

The semidisplacement powerboat on the U section shows less beam than a planing hull and, as a rule, has more deadrise. Like a semidisplacement chine hull, it has a fairly deep forefoot, fine entrance, and moderately wide transom to ensure easy lines for economical operation in speed/length ratios of 1.5 to 2.5. The keel has moderate rocker and rises aft so the transom is only lightly immersed to avoid dragging a heavy wake.

When used in a planing powerboat, the U shape may give better rough-water ability with less pounding than a typical warped-bottom hull, but at the expense of speed and economy. The round-bilge planing hull must copy the features of the V-bottom planing boat: a wide transom, fairly low deadrise to provide lift, little or no rocker in the hull aft of midships, convex forward sections to reduce pounding, and flaring topsides forward to keep the decks dry.

FIGURE 2-10

Round-bilge hull shapes.

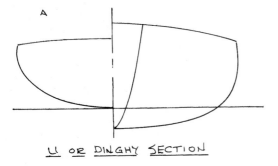

A

U OR DINGHY SECTION

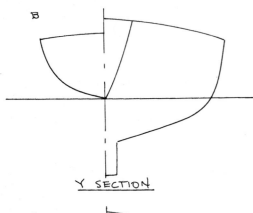

B

Y SECTION

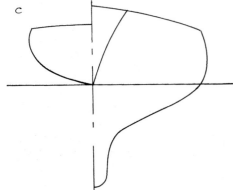

C

WINEGLASS SECTION HULL
WITH TUMBLEHOME TOPSIDES
AND FLARED BOW

The wide transom contributes to steering problems in a heavy sea, so the round-bilge planing hull must be fitted with an efficient skeg.

The Y section (Figure 2-10B) is seen in large sailing auxiliaries and motorsailers as well as slow-speed displacement powerboat hulls such as tugs, trawlers, fishing vessels, and oceangoing motoryachts. Sailing craft carry a large percentage (30% to 50%) of their displacement as ballast to contribute to stability and seaworthiness. The ballast may be all inside, as seen on some motorsailers and cruising yachts, but normally most of the ballast is fitted outside (or inside the fin of a metal or fiberglass boat) in the form of iron or lead castings.

In recent years there has been a surge of interest in heavy offshore motoryachts styled after trawlers and other workboats. These vessels utilize a deep-Y section to provide a seaworthy hull capable of long offshore passages. Usually ballast is fitted in the form of cement poured in place, often over scrap iron or lead. The hulls of these workboat yachts show a deep forefoot running into a long, straight keel, ample beam, and a fine entrance. The transom is usually relatively narrow and not deeply submerged in order to ensure a clean wake at low speeds. The double-ended hull is not uncommon. Such craft require only modest power to attain their displacement-hull speeds, and with an economical, slow-turning diesel engine combined with large fuel capacity, they can remain at sea for days in almost any weather.

The wineglass section is a modification of the Y section with the hull bottom faired in to the keel (Figure 2-10C). It is not often seen on modern sailboats but was very common 20 to 30 years ago on the long-keeled hulls of that era. The shape reduces wetted surface and turbulence at the tuck, where the hull meets the keel. It is more difficult to build than the Y section, particularly in a planked wooden boat or metal hull, but offers no real problems in fiberglass.

Wild Thing is well named. This aluminum 60-footer is intended for an around-the-world race. One look at those wide, flat stern sections tells you she was built for more-than-ordinary sailboat speeds.

A handsome sedan cruiser on a Downeast-style hull with a U-shaped midsection by Covey Island Boat Works. This is a semi-displacement boat.

The Radius-Bilge Hull

The radius-bilge hull is seen in metal displacement yachts, both sailing and power. It is an attempt to simplify construction while still producing a hull that appears to have round bilges. Basically, the hull lines are the same as a single-chine V-bottom hull, but a very large radius is introduced from bow to stern along the chine (Figure 2-11). On a typical 40-foot sailboat this bilge radius might be 2 feet at the stern increasing gradually to 4 or 5 feet at the bow. One advantage of this design is slightly reduced resistance, since the turbulence at the chine is eliminated. The biggest advantage, though, is the improved appearance and the substantially higher resale value compared to that of a chine hull. There is more labor in a radius-bilge hull, but material costs are only slightly greater. The technique is within the ability of an amateur builder, and home craftsmen have achieved excellent results on vessels of 50 feet or more.

FIGURE 2-11
A radius-bilge hull is difficult to tell from a true round-bilge.

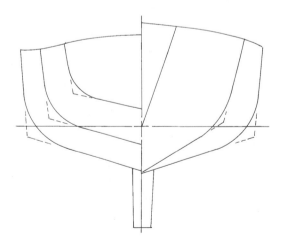

Nomad *shows how closely a radius-bilge metal hull resembles a completely formed round-bilge vessel.*

Multihulls

Multihulls have been growing rapidly in popularity. They are often thought of as new boats, but the design actually goes back hundreds of years to the time when the South Sea islanders were making their first explorations. The multihull's popularity in the past few years can be linked to its speed, stability, and in some contemporary craft, to its wide deck space and general roominess. The speed of the multihull is a result of its great stability combined with a light, unballasted hull.

The safety of multihulls has come under fire from time to time. It is generally accepted that a lightweight multihull tends to float over big seas and is spared the crushing force of breaking crests, but it can be flipped over in very high seas, a condition from which there is no recovery. Occasional stories in yachting magazines telling of capsized multihulls and their crews' struggle to stay alive on the upside-down hulls have not added to the multihull's reputation for safety.

For many years, though, the average multihull was an amateur-built craft, quite often of simple plywood construction and, too often, not very well built. A study showed that nearly half of these home-built craft were built by people with little or no boatbuilding or sailing experience. This probably accounts for much of the safety criticism. Designers such as Dick

Newick, Kurt Hughes, and others have done much to improve the design and construction of the multihull in recent years, and today's designs, even those intended for amateur construction, are a far cry from the multihulls of 15 or 20 years ago.

Multihull sailing yachts are now being produced by several fiberglass production builders as well, but the few designs I have seen seem to be more concerned with providing accommodations than providing performance. Kurt Hughes has a sound reputation for designing fast multihulls and is a believer in wide beam for stability and performance. It is interesting that he uses a 20-foot 2-inch beam on a 30-foot catamaran while a 30-foot fiberglass production catamaran has a 14-foot 6-inch beam. On his 36-footer Hughes incorporates 24 foot of beam, while a production 35-footer has only a 15-foot beam. The wide beam contributes greatly to stability. I expect the Hughes designs sail circles around the narrower production boats in any kind of a breeze. In addition,

The F-27 Sport Cruiser trimaran features a 19-foot beam, a 4-foot 11-inch draft (board down), and is fast, beachable, and trailerable.

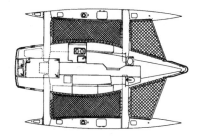

HULL SHAPES

The Glacier Bay 24 is a smooth-riding and fast power catamaran. She provides weekending accommodations and is great for picnicking, fishing, and beach cruising.

at least one FRP production catamaran has a rather strange third pod between the hulls, probably an attempt to gain standing headroom. This makes it an unusual beast, to say the least.

The very wide beam of the multihulls, even the 14½-foot-wide 30-footer, makes it difficult to find a marina slip. In my marina you may have to rent a 35- to 40-foot slip for your 30-foot multihull.

Trimarans have been designed with folding or demountable amas (amas are the outer hulls that provide stability for the fairly narrow trimaran hull) to fit onto highway trailers or into marina slips. This is essential, as trimarans are even beamier than catamarans. For example, a Hughes 37-foot trimaran designed for performance cruising has a beam of 29 feet 9 inches. Despite their large beam, trimarans, with their relatively narrow hulls, lack the roomy accommodations of catamarans, and are often more cramped below than monohulls.

Multihulls are spreading into the powerboat field now as well. High-speed catamarans are used in ferry services all over the world. Power catamarans have been designed by Hughes, Arthur Edmonds, and others. One production fiberglass power catamaran is the Glacier Bay 24, an attractive and fast daycruiser and overnighter. There is no doubt that we will see many more catamaran motoryachts in the future.

Multihulls are a different breed. If you believe that one of them might be your dream boat, you should investigate it thoroughly before making the move. Closely examine as many as you can, and if possible, charter one that meets your needs.

CHAPTER THREE

Interpreting the Lines Drawing

B efore we can examine the features of various hull shapes the reader needs to understand the lines drawing as well as the terms architects use to describe its parts. The lines drawing is the naval architect's means of depicting a three-dimensional object on paper. Three examples are shown here: a 32-foot flat-bottom sharpie, a fast 28-foot 6-inch V-bottom motorboat designed for sheet plywood planking, and a 42-foot wineglass-section sailing yacht—the popular Whitby 42.

The lines drawing shows the boat in three different views.

The *profile* is the view from the side and shows the hull above and below water. The *plan* view is the boat as seen from above. Only one side is shown, since, with a little luck and skill, the builder will make both halves of the boat the same. The third perspective, the end view, is called the *body plan*, or sometimes the *sections*. These depict vertical slices through the hull at intervals established by the designer along the LWL. Again, only half of the hull is shown, the right side being the sections forward of midships, as a general rule, and the left side being the aft sections.

The sheerline shows on all lines drawings and is

the shape of the deck as seen from the side in the profile view. It is labeled sheer in the profile view and on the plan view. In the latter view the line is really the deck edge, but it is labeled sheer so the builder is not confused by two different terms indicating the same point on the boat. When a yachtsman raves about a certain boat having a beautiful sheer, he is talking about the appearance in the profile view, not the plan view.

The chine on a hard-chine hull is the intersection of the topside and bottom planking. For a flat-bottom boat the *chine* line is shown in all three views, but the chine in the profile view also represents the centerline of the hull. The chine line of the V-bottom hull is higher than the hull centerline, of course, due to the hull's deadrise. The *fairbody* line (Figure 3-2) is the intersection of the bottom planking with the keel or skeg. On the Deer Isle 28 the keel or skeg is slab sided, so the fairbody shows as a straight line on the plan view and sections. Y-section hulls also show the fairbody line, but it may be shaped on the plan view (wider amidships and tapering toward the ends) to increase strength to support a ballast keel, heavy engines, and so forth.

These few lines—the sheer, chine, fairbody, and keel (or skeg, as it may be called)—are perfectly visi-

FIGURE 3-1

The lines drawing of Mystic, *a double-ended sharpie yacht.*

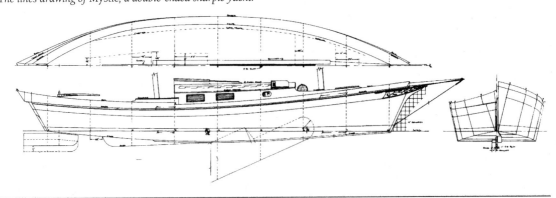

FIGURE 3-2

The Deer Isle 28 is a fast V-bottom powerboat designed for sheet plywood construction.

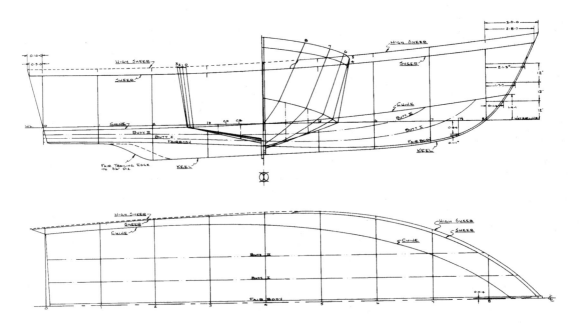

ble on any hard-chine hull at the nearest boatyard. Simple flat-bottom boats like the sharpie, and V-bottom hulls without any curvature in the sections, require only these few lines to depict the hull shape. However, on vessels with more intricate hull form, such as round-bottom boats or chine hulls with curved sections, the builder needs to know the shape of the boat between these points. The designer establishes this by means of additional lines called *waterlines, buttocks,* and *diagonals.*

FIGURE 3-3
The Whitby 42 lines show a modern, full-keel cruiser.

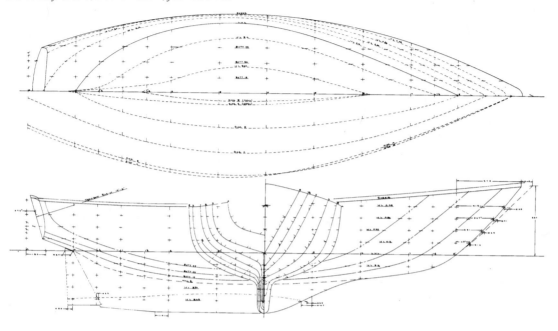

The V-bottom powerboat lines show a slightly more complex hull because it was designed for sheet plywood planking. For this reason, the boat has curvature in the forward sections due to the conical projection as the sheet plywood is twisted to form the increasing deadrise forward. The designer draws in buttocks to enable the builder to loft this curved shape full size and saw out the frames. Buttocks are vertical slices through the hull parallel to the centerline. They show as straight lines in the plan view and on the body plan, but as long, gently curved lines on the profile view.

The lines drawing of the auxiliary sailing yacht shows three buttocks and also includes waterlines (Figure 3-3). These are slices drawn through the hull parallel to the LWL to better define the boat's more complex shape. It is as if the hull was sliced like a layer cake, with each waterline representing the outline of one of the layers. The waterlines show as straight lines in the profile and section views but as long curved lines on the plan view. On the Whitby 42 the LWL is drawn solid, and the waterlines above and below water are dashed for clarity.

The final fairing lines used on the auxiliary drawing are the *diagonals*. These are shown as angled lines on the body plan where they intersect as many stations as possible at close to a 90-degree angle. They are usually laid out across from the plan view and appear as long, easy curves. Some designers consider the diagonals to be the most important lines when fairing the hull of a sailing yacht because they most closely resemble the shape of the water flow when the boat is sailing at a good angle of heel.

The lines drawing, whether drawn by hand or created on a computer, as is often the case today, is done to a rather small scale, from $\frac{1}{10}$ to $\frac{1}{24}$ actual size. The builder, however, needs to have the hull lines full size in order to make the frames or molds for the boat. Many builders still get down on their hands and knees on a large floor and redraw the lines full size from a table of dimensions (called offsets) provided by the designer. With computers, however, it is possible to have a plotter draw the lines full size from a CAD (computer-aided design) program. This can save the builder considerable time and sore knees. The drawing can be done on paper, but this may create problems because paper patterns can stretch and shrink with changes in humidity. Mylar is preferred by many builders, as it is a stable material and ensures accurate lofting.

Now that we've introduced the lines drawing views, let's see how to interpret them. These drawings are not mute; they have secrets to tell about a boat's likely seaworthiness, comfort, and performance. Chapter 4 concerns hull profiles, so we'll postpone that discussion and instead start with the body plan.

The Body Plan

Beam

Beam is, perhaps, the first and most important body-plan characteristic to consider. It is obvious that a beamy hull has more interior space than its narrower sister, but there are many other ways in which beam affects the design.

The stability of a boat increases with an increase in beam. This must be qualified by pointing out that hulls of similar overall beam can vary widely in stability. Figure 3-4 shows two examples having the same beam at the deck. The boats on the right have a wide waterline beam and possess great initial stability. They will be stiff, with a snappy roll in beam seas. The boats on the left have maximum beam at the deck and are quite narrow at the LWL. These boats are tender and have a tendency to roll

FIGURE 3-4

These boats have the same beam at the deck.

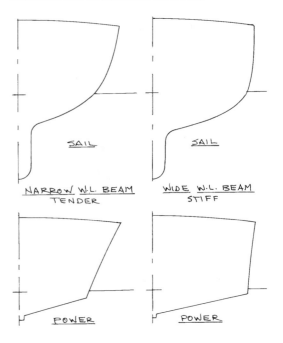

slowly but to greater angles in beam seas.

Stability is also affected by the underwater hull shape. Hard bilges or chines combined with low-deadrise angles contribute to initial stability, and give the vessel a snap roll (Figure 3-5). Softer bilges, steep deadrise, and a slack garboard indicate a more tender hull. The hull shape of a sailing yacht is not the sole criterion for determining stability, though, since the amount and location of the ballast is a major factor and must be given equal consideration.

With a displacement motorboat, or a planing hull operating at displacement speeds, wide beam increases resistance and is detrimental to performance and fuel economy. Long, narrow hulls are more easily driven at slower speeds and have an easier motion as a rule. But the planing hull is a different story. A moderate increase in beam lowers the resis-

FIGURE 3-5
Hard versus slack sections.

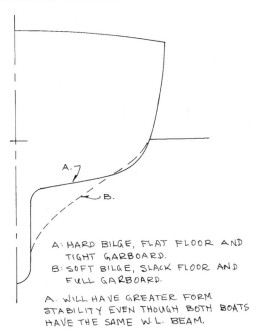

A: HARD BILGE, FLAT FLOOR AND
   TIGHT GARBOARD.
B: SOFT BILGE, SLACK FLOOR AND
   FULL GARBOARD.

A. WILL HAVE GREATER FORM
STABILITY EVEN THOUGH BOTH BOATS
HAVE THE SAME W.L. BEAM.

tance at planing speeds by adding more lift. The greater beam increases performance and fuel economy as a result, but may degrade comfort and ability in heavy weather. Beam/LWL ratios of .30 to .36 are common in modern small and mid-size planing yachts, although ratios up to .4 can be seen. For rough-water usage the lower ratios are preferred. The very large megayachts, which commonly go offshore, may have beam/LWL ratios in the .23 to .26 range to improve their behavior in heavy seas.

As was pointed out earlier, wide beam increases stability, but excess stability can adversely affect the comfort and seaworthiness of the vessel. Many chine-hull powerboats, with their great beam, wide transoms, low-deadrise bottoms, and extremely hard bilges, have such great initial stability that they almost jerk the crew and guests off their feet with a quick, snappy roll in certain wave conditions, whether at sea or at anchor. For offshore work the easier, slower motion imparted by round bilges, lower beam/LWL ratios, and reasonable deadrise is much preferable.

Of course, even a round-bilge boat can be uncomfortable. In one case, a trawler yacht with an uncomfortably quick roll was cured by adding ballast up high beneath the deck. This raised the center of gravity, reduced the stability of the boat, and slowed the roll. It is a trick that was used commonly in coastal trading schooners at the turn of the century. In a calm with rolling swells, the skipper hoisted weights to the mastheads to ease the motion.

The story is different for sailing craft. Except in a dead calm, as noted above, the added stability of wider beam does not greatly reduce motion comfort because the wind pressure on the sails has a steadying effect and slows the roll. Also, the sailboat benefits from added stability in two ways. First, it reduces the angle of heel in a breeze, and this in turn increases the effective sail area and improves the driving force of the sails. Since the area of the sails presented to the wind is reduced as the boat heels, a vessel with 1000 square feet of sail heeling at 25 degrees actually presents only 906 square feet of sail to the wind. At a 15-degree heel angle the effective area increases to 966 square feet, a 6.6% jump in sail area and, hopefully, a substantial increase in speed. Second, the reduced heel angle means that the fin or keel is more upright, increasing the efficiency of the fin, the area of the lateral plane, and the boat's draft. All of these work to increase hydrodynamic efficiency and minimize leeway.

The benefits of greater beam must be balanced against the increased resistance of the wider hull, especially when sailing to windward in choppy seas. There may also be penalties of heavier steering when running or reaching in heavy weather. The beamier vessel also has greater wetted surface, and this increases drag and reduces speed in light airs. Still, the added stability allows her to carry a larger sail plan; this can overcome the extra resistance. It is the interaction of these factors—resistance, stability, and driving force—that contributes greatly to keeping sailboat design an art rather than an exact science.

Beam/LWL ratios of sailing yachts have ranged widely over the years due to changes in the racing handicap rules. What is popular today may not be tomorrow. Because stability varies as the cube of the length, while heeling moment varies as the square of the length, larger yachts can usefully employ finer hulls, although no one ratio can be described as ideal.

In the 1890s, beam/LWL ratios as low as .16 were seen on English cutter yachts, but the beam of the average yacht has widened over the years. Today ratios of .4 and greater are not uncommon.

Section Shapes

We have discussed the general shape of the sections with relation to beam and stability, but the sections at the aft end of the LWL need some consideration, particularly in sailboats. Hard-bilged quarters with low deadrise and the bilges close to the waterline pick up waterline area and increase stability as the boat heels. But they may cause hard steering, turbulence, and related drag when the vessel is heeled to the point where the bilge is submerged. On the other hand, excessively slack quarters with steep deadrise and soft bilges do not pick up stability as the yacht heels, and the vessel may lack the power to carry sufficient sail in heavy breezes.

In sailing boats, then, the shape of the aft quarters should relate to the hull. Narrow, deep yachts that normally sail at great angles of heel should have more deadrise and slacker bilges aft to reduce resistance. Beamy, shoal hulls that do not sail on their ear can usefully employ harder bilges aft with flatter deadrise

to provide greater bearing and increased stability as the vessel heels.

In judging stern shapes you must consider that for some years the IOR (International Offshore Rule) racing-handicap rule encouraged very narrow, pinched-in, slack sterns. This became the fad for many cruising yachts as well, since the cruising boat builders always try to emulate what is newest and faddish. But it has nothing to recommend it, and it is now seen only on older yachts (thank goodness!). However, some of these boats make fine cruisers as they have many other merits; the pinched stern is not a reason to eliminate an otherwise good used boat from your shopping list. Today the trend is to cram in sleeping cabins aft, even under the cockpit of very small cruisers, as too many buyers equate the number of berths with the quality of the design. To provide space for these sleeping kennels, and make them as large as possible, the designers widen the sterns, sometimes to excess. The result can be difficult steering, nose diving, and broaching when the boat is driven hard in a stiff breeze. Frankly, I would rather have an old IOR pinched stern!

The aft sections in displacement powerboats are not unlike those of beamy sailboats. The quarters show low, fairly hard bilges with modest deadrise. The true-displacement powerboat, designed for speed/length ratios below 1.4, usually has a fairly narrow transom with the transom tip at or just below the LWL to create the proper prismatic coefficient for its designed speeds. In semidisplacement hulls, as the speed/length ratio increases, the transom width and depth increase, and the bilges usually are hardened to raise the Cp to the correct value for the anticipated speed. Round-bilge planing hulls have a wide transom with little deadrise and very hard bilges that are well immersed to provide bearing aft, lift for planing, and a Cp of .70 or greater.

Chine-planing hulls usually have their chines well immersed aft, with deadrise angles at the stern ranging from almost flat in some warped-bottom hulls up

FIGURE 3-6
Robert Beebe's Passagemaker, *an offshore powerboat capable of extended voyaging, has a deep full-bodied hull that cannot plane. (From* Sea Sense, *by Richard Henderson. International Marine, 1991)*

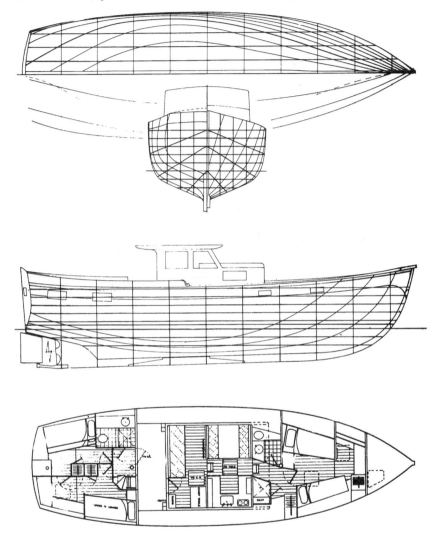

to 20 degrees in deep-V hulls. The transom is wide to provide lift at planing speeds and is generally deeply immersed at rest. Some deep-V hulls have their chines aft running at or slightly above the LWL. This indicates a boat that has reduced stability at low speeds or at anchor. Such a boat may be a great ski boat but is uncomfortable for fishing or cruising, particularly in beam seas.

INTERPRETING THE LINES DRAWING

FIGURE 3-7

Lines and arrangement of Dave Gerr's Off Soundings 34, a sportfisherman with a moderate beam and a fine deadrise forward to eliminate pounding. A wide immersed chine aft provides a very stable fishing platform. (From The Nature of Boats, by Dave Gerr. International Marine, 1992)

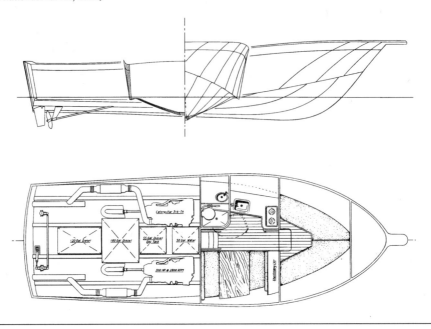

FIGURE 3-8

Ray Hunt's Vivacity, a nearly constant V design. The deadrise aft is 20 degrees, which proved a good compromise between sea-keeping and planing ability. (From Sea Sense, by Richard Henderson. International Marine, 1991)

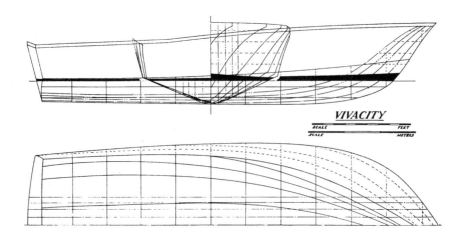

FIGURE 3-9A

Profile versus performance: Note the increase in hull draft and fore-and-aft rocker as the shape changes from planing to displacement type.

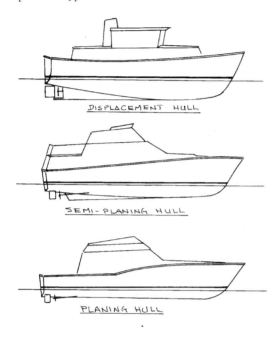

FIGURE 3-9B

While all three hulls show similar beams, they have major dissimilarities in draft and displacement.

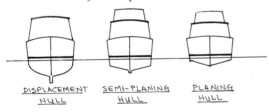

In any case, as pointed out earlier, it is desirable in a fast powerboat that the deadrise angle be about 25 degrees in the area where the boat leaves the water at planing speed and comes back down on a wave. The sections there should be convex in order that the boat mush down slowly, rather than dive quickly into the

sea only to stop just as quickly when the chine is immersed. If this 25-degree angle, or something close to it, is carried all the way to the stern of a deep-V hull, then the boat, leaping off a wave at horrendous speeds, can still land on the next sea with something less than ankle-breaking deceleration. Such performance is not for the faint of heart, obviously, and is unnecessary for the average cruiser, but it does make for a boat that can race through choppy ocean seas at high speeds.

Flam, Flare, and Topsides

Let's define these terms. Flare is a concave section in the topsides; flam is a convex section in the topsides (Figure 3-10). At least one marine dictionary disagrees and says that flam is the concave section above the waterline in the bows. Webster's, however, says that the word comes from the French *fanfelue*, a bubble. Since I have never seen a concave bubble, I continue to define flam as a convex section above the LWL.

The topsides in both sail and powerboats show either flam or flare in the sections forward of midships unless the boat is a simple, hard-chine hull with straight-line sections between the chine and deck edge. Flare is generally seen on sailing craft designed with clipper bows, since it fairs in smoothly with the overall hull shape. Given the same beam at the deck, flam sections have more reserve buoyancy and tend to make the bow rise with a sea and ride over it, rather than digging into it. Fortunately, most yachts that sail on their ear are of the older, narrower form, often having long bow and stern overhangs. The bow sections of these craft are usually of the convex or flam shape to provide extra buoyancy as the bow noses into a sea. The combination works well.

Motorboats of sheet construction, whether plywood or metal, show flam forward to facilitate fitting the sheet material around the hull in construction. A

FIGURE 3-10
Flam, flare, and tumblehome.

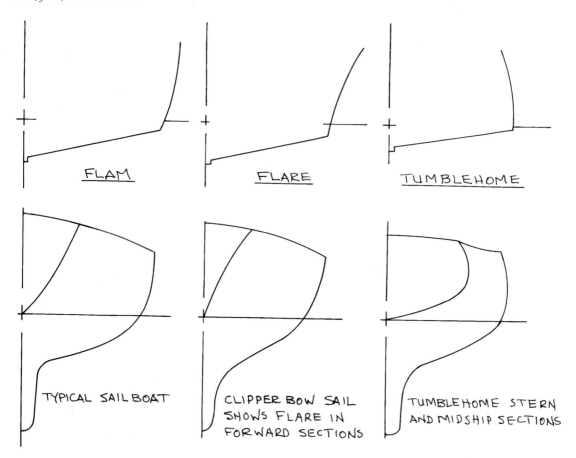

flammed section does not throw off spray as well as flared sections, but a good spray rail at the chine goes a long way to offset this rather minor fault. Still, the average planked wood or fiberglass motoryacht shows flare in the forward sections in order to keep spray down and fit with the general aesthetics and style of the vessel. This may be continued all the way to the stern, as in the ruggedly handsome Huckins yachts of bygone years, or it may be reduced gradually to zero toward midships and change into flam from there aft.

Toward the stern of a powerboat the sections often curve inward so far that the deck becomes narrower than the LWL; this is termed *tumblehome*. The shape has no real advantages for a powerboat but does prevent the deck edges from grinding together when two craft are rafted side by side. The disadvantages include a narrower cockpit and reduced buoyancy in extreme following seas. There is no good reason to use the shape except, perhaps, for personal ideas of aesthetics. A well-designed tumblehome stern can be very pretty indeed on the right boat.

FIGURE 3-11
A 17-foot 7-inch round-bottomed wooden launch that has been built by numerous backyard and professional builders. (From Boatbuilding Manual, *by Robert Steward. International Marine, 1987)*

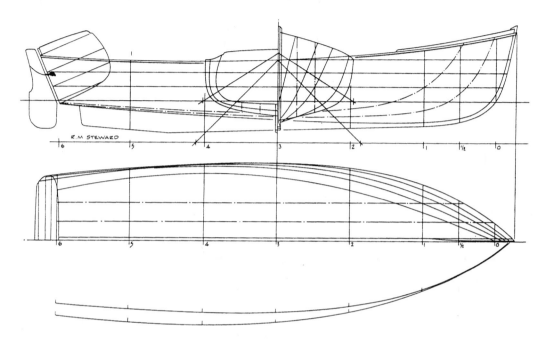

In past years the IOR rule encouraged substantial tumblehome amidships in racing sailing yachts, and some designers went to extremes—as some designers always do. The advantages of great tumblehome were a wide beam at the measurement points that improved the handicap, plus a relatively narrow deck that reduced weights high up in the hull and lowered the center of gravity. On the other hand, the stability is reduced when such a boat heels to extreme angles in a squall, and the working space on deck can be cramped. Fortunately, this is another trend that has died by the wayside. Tumblehome toward the stern sections of a sailboat does not have anywhere near the drawbacks of excess tumblehome amidships, and it can result in quite handsome counters and transoms. The sterns of the handsome Friendship sloops are a nice example of tumblehome aft. Bob Perry has also done some very good work on double-enders with moderate tumblehome in the stern sections and reverse canoe sterns in profile view. Like anything else, this can be carried to extremes; we have seen examples by other designers that are nothing short of ridiculous.

Freeboard

There is a tendency today toward greater freeboard in vessels of all types, except perhaps canoes and rowboats. Freeboard, defined as the distance between the LWL and the deck, is an important factor in both sail and powerboats. Generally, unless a boat has an extremely high center of gravity or excessive tumblehome, its stability increases with the angle of heel until the deck edge submerges. After that the stability decreases to zero at the capsize point. Thus, higher freeboard provides a bank of reserve stability that you can draw on as the boat heels in extreme conditions. Obviously on an open boat, whether sail or power, the higher the freeboard the farther the boat can heel before water starts to slop dangerously over the gunwale; high freeboard can be a lifesaver at times. Good freeboard in open boats also allows the boat to carry a greater load of people or stores.

Substantial freeboard in a powercraft assures a drier boat when nosing into a chop and, more important, a boat that does not take solid water across her decks when driven into a head sea. Similarly, freeboard carried well aft does much to prevent *pooping* (a breaking wave coming in over the stern and flooding the boat) when running before a very steep sea or passing through a breaking inlet.

On a cruising or racing sailboat it is rarely possible to provide sufficient freeboard to keep the deck edge from burying when the yacht is hard pressed in a stiff wind, but it is desirable to have sufficient freeboard so the deck does not bury at moderate heel angles. Too low a freeboard may mean that green water sweeps over the lee rail at relatively low angles of heel, creating added turbulence and resistance as well as a danger to the crew. The advantages of freeboard carried well aft apply both to sailboats and to powerboats. I have been pooped once in mid-ocean—an unpleasant experience to say the least and to be avoided if at all possible.

As stated earlier, though, excessively high freeboard can be a danger if it is combined with a narrow, light, shoal hull such as a sharpie. It raises the center of gravity of the boat, possibly reducing stability to a dangerous degree, and it increases the wind's heeling effect. This dangerous combination can lead to a capsize. In addition, the area of the higher top-sides adds windage, acting as an unwanted sail and potentially creating difficulty docking or steering in crosswinds. In general, high freeboard is best suited to heavier, deeper, or beamier hulls, and is definitely out of place on light, narrow, or shoal cruisers. In such craft it is to be avoided as you would avoid a lead-filled life jacket.

The Plan View

The plan view consists of the deck edge (the sheer) and the waterlines. Let's consider sailing yachts first, as a larger variety of shapes exist and the waterlines may assume somewhat more importance than they do in the average powerboat.

As far back as the 18th century, British boat designers favored the so-called cod's-head-and-mackerel-tail shape (Figure 3-12A). This design had full, blunt waterlines forward and fine waterlines at the stern. The shape was abandoned in British ocean racers after the fiasco of the 1960 America's Cup, when the U.S. defender handily beat the full-bowed British 12-meter yacht *Sceptre* in every race of the series. The shape's disadvantage is that the overly full bow creates unnecessary resistance, particularly when driving to windward in choppy seas. In the 1930s a balanced bow and stern shape (Figure 3-12B) was advanced as the answer to obtaining better helm balance when driving to windward in a stiff breeze. This design had a slightly finer bow and fuller stern than the "cod's head and mackerel tail"; although an improvement, it did not produce a fast boat. However, it does steer beautifully because the hull does not change shape greatly with increased angles of heel.

Figure 3-12C shows the wedge shape, which has been widely used in America for years and is still seen in the majority of contemporary designs. The entry at the bow is fine, often straight, the widest sec-

FIGURE 3-12

The plan view.

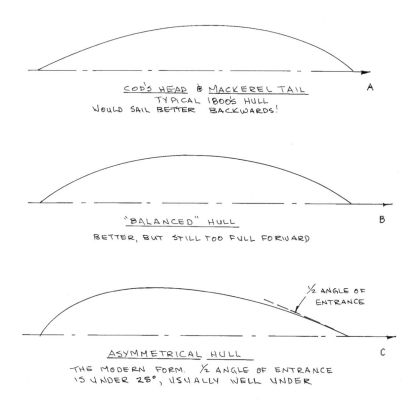

COD'S HEAD & MACKEREL TAIL
TYPICAL 1800's HULL
WOULD SAIL BETTER BACKWARDS!

A

"BALANCED" HULL
BETTER, BUT STILL TOO FULL FORWARD

B

½ ANGLE OF
ENTRANCE

ASYMMETRICAL HULL
THE MODERN FORM. ½ ANGLE OF ENTRANCE
IS UNDER 25°, USUALLY WELL UNDER

C

tion is abaft midships at about 55% of the LWL, and the stern is quite full. It has been said that the shape promotes excessive rounding up with a fierce weather helm when driven hard to windward, but unless carried to extremes, this rarely shows up in practice and the design has proven fast and weatherly. Incidentally, *weatherly* means that the vessel performs well to windward and has nothing to do with seaworthiness.

The forward waterlines have been sharpened in the past 20 years as the LWL has become progressively longer in relation to the LOA. Half angles of entrance (the angle that the LWL makes with the hull centerline) of 25 degrees or more were the norm on the shorter waterline yachts of the 1960s, but angles of 20 degrees and less are commonly seen today. These forward waterlines should be straight or slightly convex; hollow waterlines should be avoided when possible. Some boats, notably those with deep forefoots and plumb bows such as catboats and clipper-bowed craft, show a marked hollow in the forward waterlines, but this is acceptable because it cannot be avoided if their diagonals are not to be overly full.

As the forward waterlines approach the deck they become increasingly full, although racing yachts tend to have relatively fine deck lines in order to keep weight in the ends minimal. Cruisers need more fullness because the added hull volume provides reserve buoyancy to lift the heavier weights of stores, chain, anchors, and gear when the boat is driving into heavy seas. A full deck-line also tends to keep the decks dry and provides a wider working platform, so it makes good sense on an out-and-out cruising yacht.

Displacement motorboats have the maximum beam at or just forward of midships, and the forward waterline shapes resemble those of the sailing yacht. The lines are fairly fine forward and double-ended or almost double-ended aft, similar to the lines of a sailboat. Cruising motoryachts may have slight fullness forward because the added resistance this creates is not as serious as it is in sailboats due to the reserves of power available. In some displacement hulls designed for speed/length ratios below 1.34, and where economy of operation is critical, a prismatic coefficient of .54 is desirable. This requires fine ends, as in sailing craft, with half angles of entrance as tight as possible. Like the sailing yacht, the waterlines on powerboats fill out as the deck level is approached, and the deckline itself may be very full indeed, almost rounded. This keeps spray down when motoring into a chop and provides added interior volume, greater deck space, and reserve buoyancy.

Semiplaning and planing powerboats usually have their maximum beam somewhat ahead of midships, and their forward waterlines may be quite full. These boats get up at speed and ride over the seas, so they do not require the fine waterlines of displacement powerboats. Semiplaning (or semidisplacement) hulls generally show a narrowing of the waterlines or chine aft from the maximum beam to the transom because this gives a prismatic coefficient suitable to their low- to medium-speed performance. On the other hand, high-speed planing hulls carry their width aft to the transom with little or no narrowing of the waterlines or chine. This provides the maximum area for lift at planing speeds, but the wide stern can cause steering problems when motoring

before heavy seas at low speeds. A good-sized skeg alleviates this problem greatly.

Buttocks

The buttock lines that we are concerned with in sailing yachts are the *quarter buttocks*, those about 25% of the beam out from the centerline and in the aft quarter. Sailboats should show easy buttocks without excess rounding up in the quarters. Modern, light-displacement racing yachts, with their wide, flattish transoms carried low to the LWL, have extremely long, straight, and easy buttocks indeed when compared with older, heavier hulls. Modern racing sailboats can achieve very high speeds when reaching and running as a result and are generally faster to windward as well.

Moderate-displacement sailboats with their deeper, heavier hulls show more rounding in the aft buttocks. Still, the run should be as straight as possible for about one-eighth to one-quarter of the waterline length forward of the aft end of the LWL. At this point it fairs easily into the midship sections. The very husky double-ender of the old Colin Archer or Tahiti type had heavily rounded buttocks aft, but this produces a slow boat due to the short, steep run. Also, such craft may be prone to dragging a large quarter wave, which creates considerable extra resistance, and their short, narrow ends may lack reserve buoyancy and so be subject to pooping in extreme conditions.

Displacement motorboats have buttock lines that resemble those of the modern racing sailboat aft, rising from midships to a transom that is only lightly, if at all, immersed. The heavier the displacement of the boat, the steeper the buttock lines aft, because they rise from a deep midship section to a shoal transom. When a higher speed/length ratio is required, in the range of semidisplacement speeds, the midship sec-

FIGURE 3-13
Note how the buttock lines of the fast, fin-keel Whitby 55 are considerably flatter in the stern quarters than those of the relatively heavier Whitby 42.

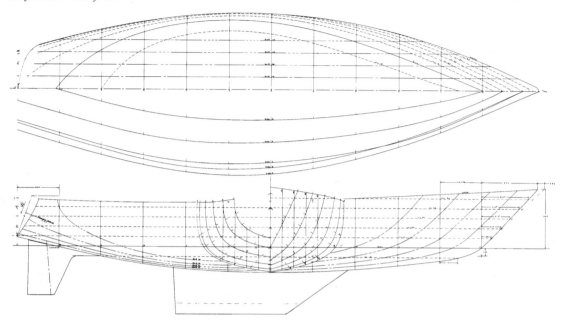

tion tends to be shallower due to the lighter displacement, and the transom becomes more deeply immersed, flattening the buttock lines so they become more conducive to the higher speeds. The smaller midship section and deeper transom also increase the prismatic coefficient, which, as we have seen, is essential to efficiency as speeds increase.At speed/length ratios of 2 and over, the buttock lines become very flat indeed, virtually parallel to the waterline, with little or no curvature abaft midships. Full-planing boats have a fairly shoal midship section and deep transom to keep the buttock and chine lines straight and parallel to the waterline, or even running downward at a slight angle as they continue aft to the transom. Again, this affects the prismatic coefficient and raises it to the .70 and higher figures required for planing speeds.

Diagonals

Diagonals are primarily fairing lines and, as such, are an aid to the designer in creating the hull lines and to the builder in lofting the lines full size. The lines drawing of the Whitby 42 (Figure 3-3), for example, shows a typical set of diagonals that were used for fairing the hull lines both on the drawing and on the full-size lofting. The shape of the diagonals vary with their angle and their location in the hull. The main point the designer considers is that the diagonals be fair, smooth curves without abrupt humps or hollows. It must be noted, however, that diagonals that are placed fairly upright and close to the centerline take on shapes similar to the ends of the boat. If the ends show hard knuckled bows or bustle sterns with abrupt turns, the diagonals will

FIGURE 3-14

The opening spread of Westy Farmer's presentation of the "Tahiti," a double-ender ketch, in his 1935 edition of How to Build 20 Boats. (From A Ketch Called Tahiti, by J. Stephen Doherty. International Marine, 1987)

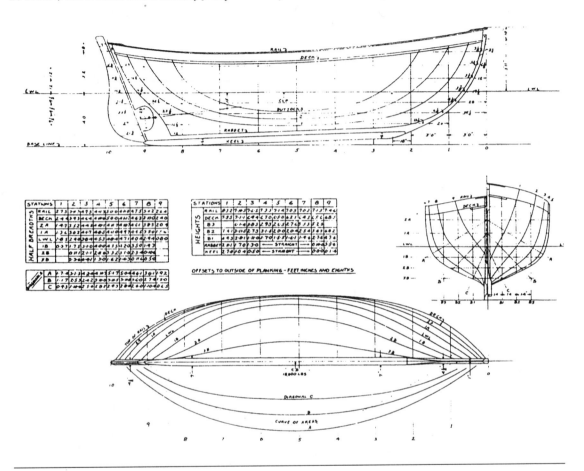

FIGURE 3-15

The Valiant 40, designed by Robert Perry, shows the rounded Baltic stern in a modern hull. Her full sections aft produce plenty of buoyancy for following seas. (From Sea Sense, by Richard Henderson. International Marine, 1991)

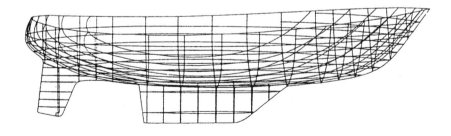

reflect this and can be disregarded as any clue to the performance of the vessel.

Modern computer design programs may place little or no emphasis on diagonals. The program that I use does not even include diagonals in the hull lines or offsets. The boats are designed and faired completely with sections, buttocks, and waterlines. Although I haven't missed the diagonals, they may be informative on some designs—for example, clipper-bowed yachts or other boats with deep forefoots.

CHAPTER FOUR

Lateral Plane

Sailboat Lateral Plane

Nathanael Herreshoff developed the fin keel around the turn of the 20th century as a way to reduce wetted surface and, thus, increase a sailboat's speed. The concept, however, was carried to extremes by later designers in an attempt to gain even more speed at the expense of balance and sea-worthiness. This gave fin-keel boats a bad reputation, and as a result, the fin keel fell out of favor for more than 50 years, except on a few smaller racing classes such as the famous Star-class sloop. In the 1960s, Bill Lapworth revived the fin keel for cruiser-racers with his very successful Cal 40 sloop. Ever since, the fin-keel, in various forms, has been the most common underbody profile.

Full Keels

Before the rediscovery of the fin keel there had been three basic underbody shapes: the full keel, the modified full keel, and the short keel. Figure 4-1A shows a traditional long keel with deep forefoot that was the rule for many years and is still seen in a few bluewater cruisers, motorsailers, and large schooners. It has the advantages of good directional stability and the ability to heave-to, but its faults include great wetted surface, inefficient lateral plane, slowness in tacking, and a general lack of handiness. Only a few hide-bound traditionalists favor this design for the average cruiser of today.

The full-keel shape was progressively shortened after Olin Stephens cut away the forefoot and the aft end on his design of the famous yawl *Dorade* in the late 1920s. *Dorade* proved very successful, winning the Transatlantic and Fastnet races shortly after her launching. Indeed, *Dorade* still sails in the Pacific Northwest and still wins classic yacht races. The cut-away forefoot and raking rudderpost, as shown in Figure 4-1B, increased handiness and reduced wet-ted surface, so the boats were faster in light air and more maneuverable. Like many good things, the cutaway keel was carried to extremes. Some inshore racers and cruisers had such short keels (Figure 4-1C) that they were extremely difficult, even danger-ous, to sail under spinnaker in any kind of a sea. These excessively short keels are not suited to racing or cruising.

A full-keel-boat of reasonable vintage with mod-erate cutaway ends can be a good performer and a

FIGURE 4-1

Full keel variations.

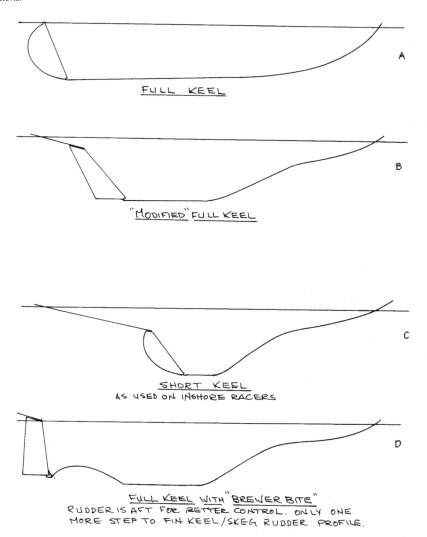

FULL KEEL   A

"MODIFIED" FULL KEEL   B

SHORT KEEL
AS USED ON INSHORE RACERS   C

FULL KEEL WITH "BREWER BITE"
RUDDER IS AFT FOR BETTER CONTROL. ONLY ONE
MORE STEP TO FIN KEEL/SKEG RUDDER PROFILE.   D

fine cruising boat. Given a reasonable handicap, it can also be a club racer, although not a front-line contender. Some examples are the Luders 33, the Alberg designs built by Cape Dory and Whitby, and, more recently, the cruising designs of Bob Harris and Bob Perry.

In my work I have used a full keel with good cutaway forward and with the rudder as far aft as possible and quite vertical in the modern style. A large cutout separates the rudder from the keel proper (Figure 4-1D). This gives a lateral plane with about the same wetted area as the older cutaway style, but with better directional stability, a higher aspect ratio for the keel, and improved handiness when maneuvering in tight quarters. Bob Perry has termed this form "the Brewer bite."

Keel-Centerboarders

The keel-centerboarder (Figure 4-5) became popular in the 1950s when the Stephens-designed *Finisterre* began its successful racing career. This form is still viable if a beamy, stable, shoal-draft cruiser is desired without sacrificing windward ability. Indeed, the Hinckley-built Bermuda 40, a keel-centerboarder designed by the late Bill Tripp, has been in production since the late 1960s and has made many long and successful voyages. The changes in the handicap system brought about by the introduction of the IOR rule in the early 1970s doomed the keel-centerboarder as a winning ocean racer. As a result, it fell out of favor and is rarely seen today.

Fin Keels

Once fin-keel yachts were rediscovered, they became so successful as ocean and inshore racers that the fin keel is now standard for cruising boats as well. The fin reduces wetted surface to a minimum and improves weatherliness, while the leverage of its aft-hung rudder provides good directional stability, ease of steering, and extreme handiness in tight quarters. For these reasons, the fin is here to stay for both cruisers and racers; it is not just another fad.

The balanced spade rudder, commonly used with the fin keel, has one serious fault. It can "stall out" and cause the loss of all steering ability if the helm is turned quickly to moderate (12- to 15-degree) angles. This can create some exciting and dangerous broaches in downwind sailing. For this reason, many designers favor a skeg-hung rudder for the cruising boat. Fitting a skeg ahead of the rudder increases the stalling angle

and reduces the chance of broaching. In addition, a propeller aperture can be fitted in a skeg of moderate size. This protects the prop from pot warps and the shaft from poorly placed haul-out slings.

One advantage of the balanced spade rudder is that it can steer the boat in reverse. No other rudder can make this claim; indeed, even skeg-hung rudders cause the boat, when reversing, to kick off to one side or the other depending on the rotation of the propeller. It might seem insignificant, but the ability to steer in reverse can make life easier in tight marina slips.

There are numerous types of fin keels (Figure 4-3), from shark-fin shapes to whale-tail shapes, and the designers all claim advantages for their favorite form. Still, the most common fin is squarish with an angled leading edge. For the average cruiser the fin is a low-aspect-ratio shape, fairly long and of moderate draft. The reason for this is that low wetted surface and high efficiency are not as important to the cruising skipper as reasonable draft and the ability to go into shoal waters. The racing yacht, on the other hand, shows a more extreme high-aspect-ratio fin, deep and narrow, to gain maximum efficiency with minimal resistance and wetted area. Some extreme ocean racers, such as the BOC around-the-world yachts, may have fins as deep as 13 to 17 feet, hardly suitable for your favorite gunkhole.

Fins are hydrodynamically shaped, of course, and the fin waterlines are usually derived from one of the NACA (National Advisory Committee for Aeronautics) shapes, which have been tested for lift and resistance at various speeds (Figure 4-4). In general, the waterlines have an elliptical leading edge and a fairly sharp trailing edge. The maximum width of the fin is located between 35% and 50% of its length aft and ranges between 10% and 15% of the fore and aft length. Every designer has a favorite NACA shape for different fin types and purposes. In truth, there is no perfect fin.

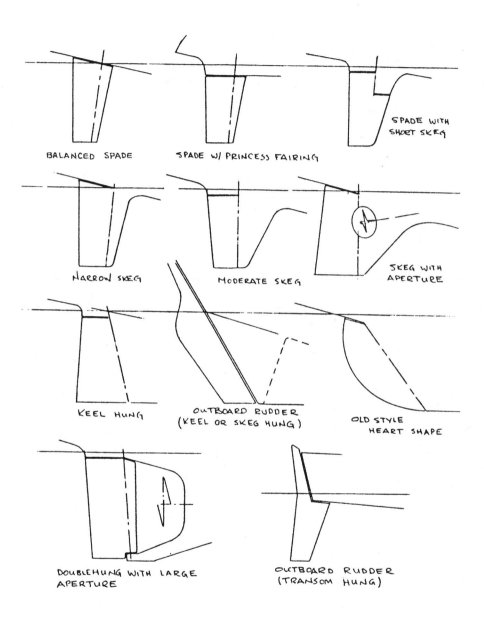

BALANCED SPADE

SPADE W/ PRINCESS FAIRING

SPADE WITH SHORT SKEG

NARROW SKEG

MODERATE SKEG

SKEG WITH APERTURE

KEEL HUNG

OUTBOARD RUDDER (KEEL OR SKEG HUNG)

OLD STYLE HEART SHAPE

DOUBLEHUNG WITH LARGE APERTURE

OUTBOARD RUDDER (TRANSOM HUNG)

FIGURE 4-3

Fin keel variations.

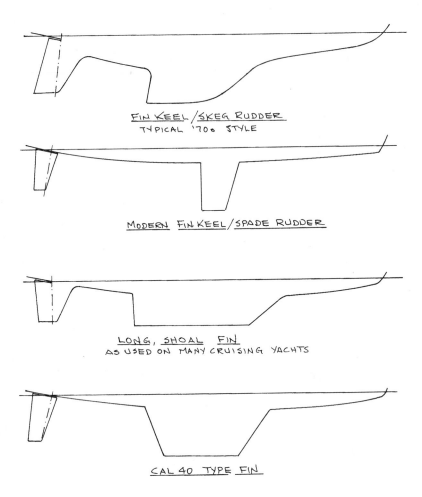

FIN KEEL / SKEG RUDDER
TYPICAL '70s STYLE

MODERN FIN KEEL / SPADE RUDDER

LONG, SHOAL FIN
AS USED ON MANY CRUISING YACHTS

CAL 40 TYPE FIN

A few yachts even have a shoal fin keel with a centerboard fitted into it, not unlike the keel-centerboarders of the 1960s. These boats are often trailer sailers, like my own Nimble Arctic 25, but a few have been built in larger, nontrailerable sizes.

Centerboarders

Today the pure centerboard (Figure 4-5) is found primarily on small daysailers or on boats designed to be trailered, although it is feasible on larger yachts as well. At the turn of the century, Commodore Ralph

FIGURE 4-4

Bulb keel variations. (From Ted Brewer Explains Sailboat Design, *by Ted Brewer. International Marine, 1985)*

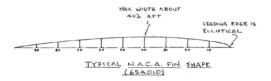

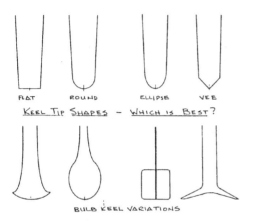

Most cruising men and women think the centerboard is too much trouble because it must be adjusted frequently when sailing if it is to be effective, and because it requires a hole in the bottom of the boat—an area of possible (probable!) trouble. The slot for the board may become jammed with rocks or barnacles. It is also awkward to paint, a source of leaks, and a home for teredos (wood-boring marine organisms) on wooden yachts. Another problem is that the centerboard trunk usually runs smack down the middle of the main cabin, effectively cutting the accommodations in two.

A few yachts sport two centerboards, a large board forward and a smaller one aft. The forward board is used primarily to reduce leeway, and the aft board is used for trim. The helm can be balanced by raising one board and lowering another to shift the center of lateral plane. This is particularly handy when sails are reefed because the change in the center of effort caused by reefing can be balanced by adjusting the boards. Of course, there are now two boards that can jam, two slots to paint, and two pendants that can break.

Bilge Boards and Leeboards

Bilge boards are simply dual boards set each side of the centerline. They are usually of high-aspect ratio, and set at an angle so the leeward board is vertical when the boat is heeled. They can be asymmetrically shaped to improve efficiency as well. This type of board eliminates the centerline trunk, and the bilge-board trunks are set into the settee fronts, which avoids splitting up the accommodations. Still, bilge boards have most of the disadvantages of twin boards, although they are not so prone to jam with rocks or mud since they sit higher in the hull. In any event, they are not popular.

Leeboards (Figure 4-8) are similar to bilge boards but are hung outside the hull. The value of this

Munroe was developing his Presto sharpie style of husky centerboarders (Figure 4-6). These handsome cruisers boasted as little as 32-inch draft on a length of 40 feet and proved to be both fast and seaworthy. Although the pure centerboard cruiser has fallen out of favor, it still has much to offer the sailor.

The Prestos, and many other centerboarders, use a long, slab-sided board, because it is economical, strong, and simple to build. However, it is not nearly as effective as a streamlined centerboard of high-aspect ratio, which provides much more lift for its area and is the only choice for a high-performance yacht. The high-aspect-ratio board does strain the trunk and hull more than the older-style centerboard, so it must be very carefully designed.

FIGURE 4-5

Centerboards and leeboards.

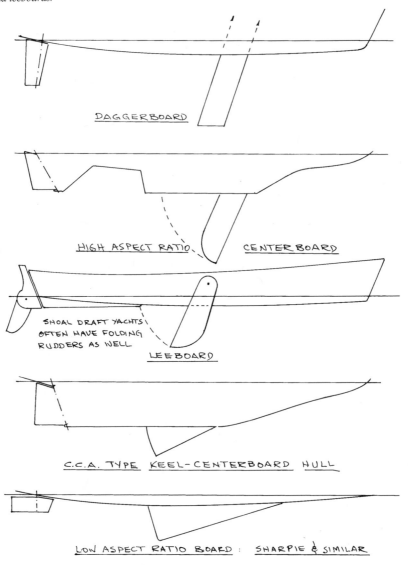

DAGGERBOARD

HIGH ASPECT RATIO   CENTERBOARD

SHOAL DRAFT YACHTS
OFTEN HAVE FOLDING
RUDDERS AS WELL

LEEBOARD

C.C.A. TYPE KEEL-CENTERBOARD HULL

LOW ASPECT RATIO BOARD : SHARPIE & SIMILAR

design is that there is nothing to leak or jam, and the boards can be painted and the pendants easily inspected. Leeboards can be asymmetrically shaped with a high-aspect ratio for increased efficiency. Although leeboards have been popular in Holland on both commercial craft and yachts for hundreds of years, they have never caught on in North America—more because of appearance than performance.

FIGURE 4-6

A Presto-style sharpie has much to offer and makes a seaworthy shoal-draft yacht.

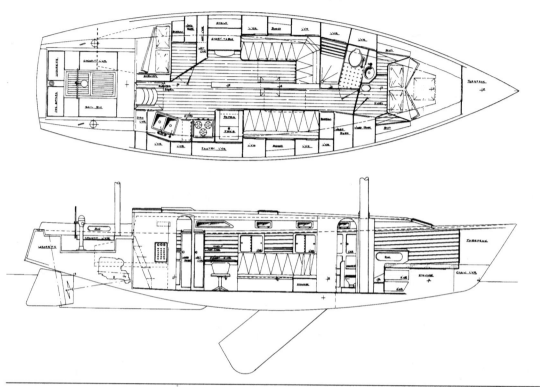

FIGURE 4-7

Twin-fin hull with asymmetrical fins.

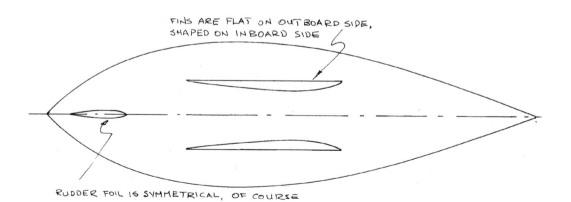

FINS ARE FLAT ON OUTBOARD SIDE, SHAPED ON INBOARD SIDE

RUDDER FOIL IS SYMMETRICAL, OF COURSE

LATERAL PLANE

FIGURE 4-8

Leeboard yachts, like the Centennial shown here, are an unusual sight in North American waters.

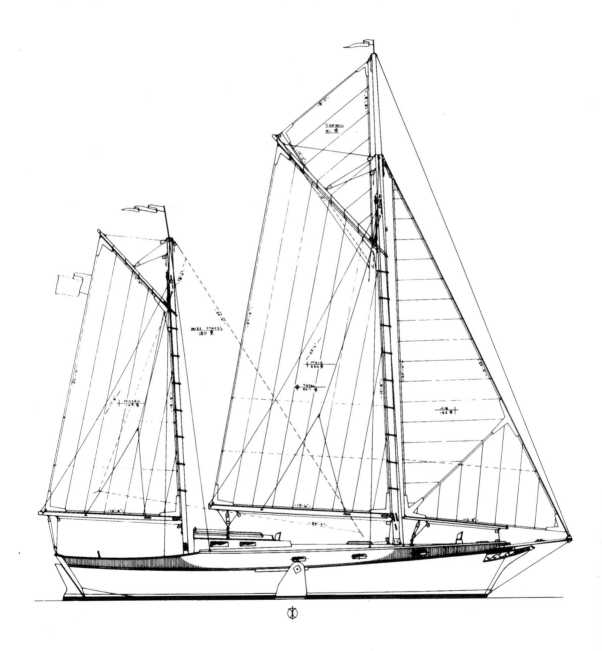

Twin Keels

Twin keels, or bilge keels, are also unpopular in North America. These dual keels set each side of the centerline have as their advantages shoal draft, and stability when grounded at low tide for bottom cleaning. Like bilge boards or leeboards, they can be asymmetrically shaped for efficiency. But bilge keels have the disadvantages of much added wetted surface and reduced stability, since the ballast is not set as low as it is with a deeper fin. In general they do not perform as well as a single fin and are rarely seen in North America. Still, bilge keels can be used to advantage on motorsailers and other cruisers where performance is secondary to convenience. They are also a good alternative to centerboards for cruising in shallow waters.

Powerboat Lateral Plane

Powerboat profiles are simpler to consider than sailboat profiles since the purpose of their lateral plane is to provide directional stability and, perhaps, propeller protection. The powerboat operates basically in a straight line, so yaw or leeway do not weigh as heavily as they do with sailboats.

Heavy-displacement powerboat hulls often resemble the old, full-keel sailing yachts but have less draft (Figure 4-9). They show a deep forefoot and a long, straight keel and usually have a single, large propeller that is well protected behind the keel. Such a boat can keep its course well, even in choppy seas.

Semidisplacement hulls should also have a fairly deep forefoot and a long skeg to provide directional

FIGURE 4-9

Powerboat lateral plane.

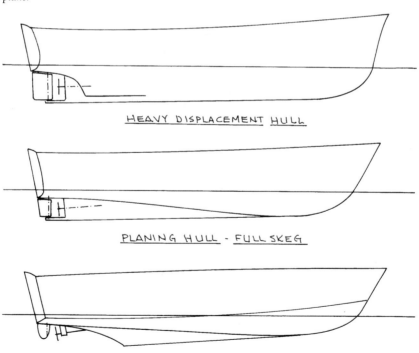

HEAVY DISPLACEMENT HULL

PLANING HULL - FULL SKEG

PLANING HULL - CUT AWAY SKEG

LATERAL PLANE

stability. The deep forefoot is desirable since it produces finer lines forward and helps to keep the bow from being knocked to leeward when traveling slowly at right angles to the wind and seas. Many semidisplacement hulls are the single-screw type and, just as in the full-displacement hull, the skeg should be carried aft so the propeller is supported and protected by the skeg or keel. On twin-screw powerboats, the skeg should be long enough and deep enough that the costly propellers are not damaged in a minor grounding.

Planing hulls obtain a great deal of directional stability from their speed, and deep planing hulls gain directional stability from their hull form as well. Still, on warped-bottom (modified V-bottom) hulls, a skeg helps to provide a steady helm during low-speed operation, particularly when running before heavy seas. If deep enough, the skeg also provides some propeller protection, even to twin-screw boats, and that is advantageous in driftwood-littered waters like those of the Northwest. Hitting even a small piece of driftwood with a high-speed prop usually means a bent blade, a costly haulout, and a fat bill for prop rebuilding.

A few twin-screw boats have twin skegs to support and protect the shafts and propellers. These create some added resistance, with small costs in speed and fuel economy, but they make good sense in many powerboats, particularly those operating in shoal- or driftwood-infested waters.

CHAPTER FIVE

Sailboat Rigs

Over the ages the rigs of fore-and-aft sailing craft have evolved through the lateen, the lugsail, the gaff, and the sliding gunter to the Bermudan (also called marconi or jibheaded) rig. Today, most rigs are either gaff or Bermudan. Other rigs are rare, except for the lateen rig, which is used on Arabian dhows and Sunfish and other small board sailers. It is rarely noted that the dipping-lug rigs used on smuggling luggers in the early 1800s were reputed to be much more weatherly than the gaff rigs of the huge customs cutters of that day. Unfortunately, the dipping-lug rig requires a large crew and is not practical on the modern yacht.

Sail Shape and Headsail Size

The Gaff Rig

There is much to be said for the gaff rig (Figure 5-1). Compared with other rigs, it has a low center of effort and a much reduced heeling moment because the sail area is spread more fore-and-aft. Having two halyards controlling the throat and peak, it is easier to adjust a poor-fitting or blown-out sail. The gaff rig is more efficient downwind than the Bermudan rig, because it presents a flatter sail to the breeze, if it is properly vanged, and in a squall the peak halyard can be let go and the sail "scandalized" to quickly reduce area. The rig uses shorter spars and simpler standing rigging, and if things go wrong at sea, as they too often do, it is easier to repair than the Bermudan. Also, the gaff rig is flexible, does not require the sensitive tuning of a Bermudan rig, and generally transfers less strain to the hull.

The disadvantages of the rig are the heavier spars and gaff, the lack of a permanent backstay and the consequent need for running backstays, and the much poorer performance to windward compared with a modern Bermudan rig. The gaff sail's low-aspect ratio and its attachment to the mast, by hoops or lacing, cannot compare with the efficiency of the high-aspect-ratio Bermudan rig with its sail track or mast slot.

The Bermudan Rig

The Bermudan (marconi, jibheaded) rig is a much better performer to windward than the gaff rig due to its higher aspect ratio, as noted. The mast and

FIGURE 5-1

Types of rigs.

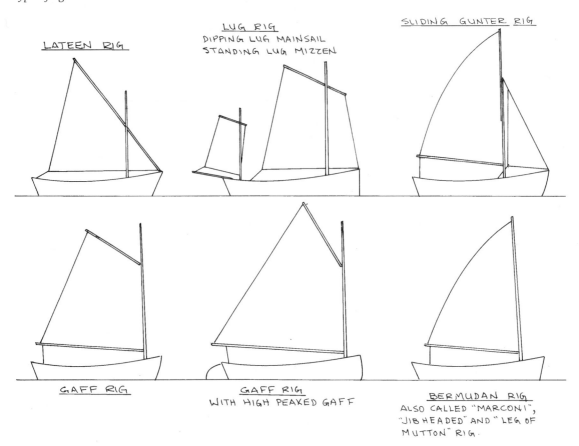

spars are much lighter for a comparable sail area, and modern developments in aluminum extrusions have given the average Bermudan rig an advantage in both weight and cost over the solid or laminated wood spars and the extensive running rigging of the gaff rig. Of course, any cost advantage will be nullified if the Bermudan rig is a racing type, with a high-tech triple-spreader setup and an inboard chainplate combination. Speed costs money. It always has.

The contemporary Bermudan rig has the safety of a permanent backstay and can be fitted with modern roller furling/reefing equipment that furls or reefs the sail into the mast or boom to simplify handling. The big advantage of the gaff rig, its off-wind performance, has been largely negated on the racing yacht by the unseamanlike symmetrical spinnaker of the Bermudan racer cruisers and the safer, saner, more easily set and doused asymmetrical spinnaker developed for cruisers in recent years.

The modern, racing Bermudan rig, with its double

or even triple spreaders, is more complex and more costly than the gaff rig. Still, with its inboard chainplates, tightly sheeted jibs, and high aspect ratio, the Bermudan rig is so much more efficient that the gaff rig has no chance on the racing circuit.

Bermudan vs. Gaff

There is a world of difference between Bermudan and gaff rigs. Racing skippers prefer the Bermudan rig, as do cruising skippers who consider performance and simplicity to be major factors in the selection of a yacht. The long-range bluewater cruising skipper, the dyed-in-the-wool character sailors with romance in their souls, may prefer a gaff-rigged vessel. Over the years, numerous people have commissioned me to design a wide variety of interesting gaff rigged boats— Cape Cod catboats, sharpies, Quoddy sloops, and a handful of schooners from 28 to 70 feet. Recently I was fortunate enough to design the 70-foot schooner *Tree of Life*, and the commission was fascinating. I hope the gaff-rig lives forever. Our waters will be dull indeed if they are ever completely taken over by Bermudan sloops with white hulls, blue stripes, and blue sail covers. There are far too many already.

Headsails

On modern sailboats, headsails include working jibs, genoas, reachers, drifters, flankers, cruising spinnakers, and 180% symmetrical spinnakers.

Much has been written about the efficiency of the large overlapping genoa and the supposed slot effect that it creates in combination with the mainsail. Wind roaring through this narrow gap is said to increase the efficiency of the mainsail and pull the boat ahead or to windward. Bullpuckey!

The fallacy of this theory is proved by the fact that when the entire sail area is measured and the genoa overlap is not "free" under the prevailing racing rule,

much costly experimentation has shown that a nonoverlapping jib and a large mainsail make the best combination. The 5.5-meter sloops worldwide, and the smaller Bainbridge Redwing class in England, are both good examples of yachts where total sail area was measured and the nonoverlapping jib proved superior. The big overlapping genoa only pays its way if the overlap is not included in the handicap rating.

A genoa with a 150% LP (LP is short for Longest Perpendicular, the distance measured perpendicular from the genoa's luff to the clew as a percentage of the length of the foretriangle base; no one has ever said that sailing-yacht handicapping was simple or made sense) is a necessity on racing yachts because boats are rated for that size sail whether they carry it or not. Not to carry a 150% genoa (Figure 5-2) on a racer gives a large advantage in sail area to your opponent. The cruiser is better off carrying a bigger mainsail and a smaller, 125% to 130% genoa. This gives the cruiser the same sail area as the racer and a more easily handled rig—devil any rating.

Reachers and drifters are cut higher and fuller than genoas, of lighter material, and with a large overlap. They are essential for racers (as are bloopers, banana staysails, and a variety of other light-air rags), but are out of place on the average cruising sailboat. The cruiser can use a lightweight flanker or gennaker (or whatever the sailmaker wants to call it) to give a little boost when reaching and running in very light air. The alternative, and I've used it often when the breeze petered out, is to start the auxiliary engine and go for broke.

Rig Types

Arguing the merits of the various rigs with another sailor is like arguing the merits of wallpapers with your spouse. The end result is much the same:

FIGURE 5-2

Reacher and genoa jibs.

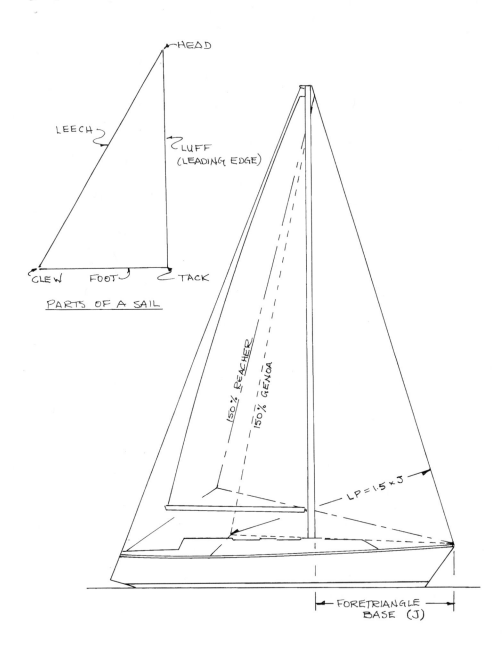

HEAD

LEECH

LUFF
(LEADING EDGE)

CLEW   FOOT   TACK

PARTS OF A SAIL

150% REACHER

150% GENOA

LP = 1.5 × J

FORETRIANGLE
BASE (J)

you get nowhere! Each rig has its diehard adherents, and they rarely switch allegiance, with the exception of the racing fraternity who change rigs with every major alteration of the handicap rules. Let's examine the various rigs.

The Catboat

The catboat (Figure 5-3) is the simplest rig to sail, but some say that it is one of the hardest to sail well.

The advantages of catboats are simplicity and excellent downwind ability. I can testify from experience in racing against modern 26- to 30-foot Bermudan-rigged catboats that they can also perform well to windward. The rig is handy and quick to get underway.

In larger cats the single huge sail can be a problem. It is difficult to raise and reef, and can be too much for the average shorthanded cruising crew.

FIGURE 5-3
Rig variations.

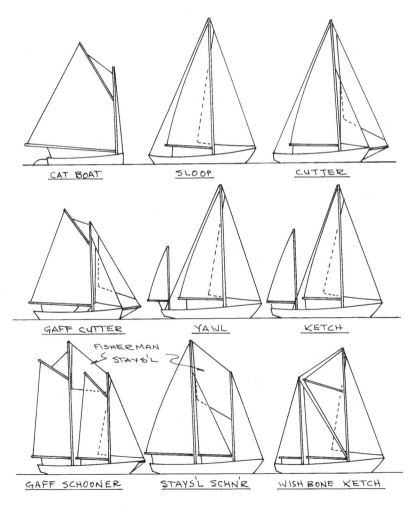

SAILBOAT RIGS

Modern Bermudan-rigged cats have proven popular in recent years because the rig does greatly simplify handling. In general, the cat rig has always been popular for small one-design sailboats (i.e., a class of sailboats built to one design so they can race together without handicap), particularly when used with a Bermudan sail. However, many sailors, and I am one of them, do not consider catboats to be a seaworthy rig for extended bluewater cruising.

The Sloop and Cutter

Originally sloops and cutters had gaff rigs with square topsails and several headsails set on a long bowsprit. The difference was that sloops were cargo carriers, while cutters were more heavily canvassed and fitted with reefing (retractable) bowsprits and topmasts to increase speed, since they were used as revenue or military craft. Today the rigs are difficult to differentiate. Generally, if the boat has only a single headsail she is a sloop, and if the mast is well aft, almost amidships, and the boat has two or more headsails, she is a cutter. The distinction becomes more confusing when the mast is forward and the boat has several headsails set on a bowsprit. Some might call her a cutter, but she is actually a double- (or triple-) headsail sloop; witness the famous Friendship sloops of Maine.

The sloop and cutter are the most weatherly of all rigs, and the ocean racing fleet is almost 100% sloop-rigged for this reason. The rigs are amply seaworthy for ocean sailing, and with modern sail-handling equipment and techniques they are safe and easy to handle in lengths up to 50 feet.

The Yawl

The yawl has been called a sloop with a mizzen. Having owned four yawls since I wrote the first edition of this book, I have developed great respect for the yawl as a cruising rig. It is almost as efficient to windward as the sloop, enables you to set an easily handled mizzen staysail to increase sail area when running or reaching in light weather, and, if you leave the mizzen up when anchored, your boat will point into the wind and not sail around her mooring. In heavier air you can drop the mainsail and the boat will balance nicely with the jib and mizzen. The yawl loses a bit to windward as the small mizzen is often more of a drag than a push, but the rig looks prettier than a sloop, and that may be a good reason to leave the mizzen set when beating.

The Ketch

The ketch has its mizzen mast stepped farther forward than the yawl and carries more sail area in the mizzen. This enables the rig to balance well under a wide variety of sail combinations. However, because the large mizzen is blanketed by the mainsail when working to windward, the ketch is the slowest of all rigs on the wind, although it partially makes up for this with its excellent reaching performance. The ketch is justly popular for cruising yachts, in which a loss of windward ability is not as important as handiness in heavy weather. Like the yawl, the ketch can set a handy and effective mizzen staysail.

The Schooner

Schooners come in endless varieties and with two, three, or more masts. The common types are the foresail schooner and the staysail schooner. If well designed, a foresail schooner can work slowly to windward in a blow with only the foresail set, thus making it a handy rig. Schooners are also excellent reaching and light-weather rigs due to the large fisherman staysail that can be set between the masts.

The old RORC (Royal Ocean Racing Club) ratings for the various rigs give a good indication of their

An Olympic 47 ketch is fitted with all roller furling sails, including a mule between the main backstay and the mizzen mast. (Peter Barlow photo)

The schooner Tree of Life *sets a fisherman staysail between her masts and a main topsail above her mainsail.*

The aluminum ketch Mystic *sets a mizzen staysail as she reaches past Diamond Head.*

efficiency and performance. Bear in mind this represents the rigs only. A gaff-rigged ketch with a well-designed hull can clobber a Bermudan sloop with an old hack of a hull.

Bermudan sloop and cutter   100%
Bermudan yawl   96%
Bermudan schooner and gaff sloop   92%
Bermudan ketch and gaff yawl   88%
Gaff schooner   85%
Gaff ketch   81%

With modern furling and reefing equipment for sail handling, there is virtually no fixed limit to rig size. Even the largest sloops can be handled with hydraulic or electric winches and furling gear—but God help the crew if something breaks down in heavy weather. For bluewater cruising, the real limit is what you and your crew can manhandle in the worst of conditions—say 40 to 45 feet for sloops, 45 to 60 feet for cutters and yawls, and any size you want for ketches and schooners, provided your crew is large enough. You can certainly go smaller and have a 23-foot yawl or a 28-foot schooner if you don't mind handling the extra strings.

Rig-Hull Relationship

The "lead" (rhymes with reed) of a sailboat is the distance that the Center of Effort (the center of the sail area) is ahead of the Center of Lateral Plane (the fore-and-aft center of the area of the hull below the LWL). It may seem that the CE should be in line with the CLP so the wind pressure exactly counters the hull's resistance to side slip, thus creating a well-balanced helm. This is not the case, however, except in a few craft with odd hulls or rigs, because as the yacht heels the CE moves to leeward while the CLP

FIGURE 5-4

Rig-hull relationship.

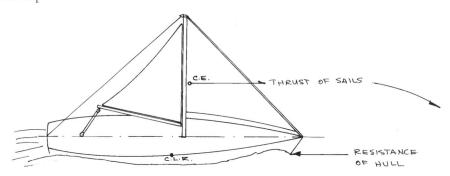

THE THRUST OF THE SAILS IS TO LEEWARD OF THE RESISTANCE OF THE HULL AND FORMS A COUPLE, TURNING THE HULL TO WINDWARD.

WITH CORRECT LEAD, THE SIDE FORCE OF THE SAILS WILL OFFSET THE LUFFING MOMENT AS SHOWN ABOVE.

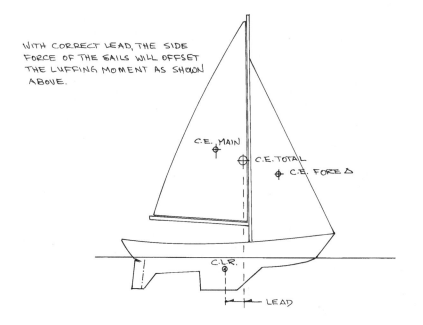

remains virtually in the same place; this creates a couple, or force, that tends to shove the vessel to windward (Figure 5-4).

The great majority of fore-and-aft rigged sailing yachts require that the CE be well forward of the CLP. This distance, the lead, is usually expressed as a percentage of the waterline length. Too little lead creates the condition called *weather helm* and requires that the rudder be turned to leeward (and the tiller to weather, thus weather helm) in order to steer a straight course. This is fatiguing to the crew and detrimental to speed. The opposite condition, lee helm, is caused by having too great a lead. It is dangerous because the vessel will not round up into the wind to relieve the pressure on her sails if the helm is left untended. A serious lee helm may make it impossible to bring the yacht about, forcing the crew to jibe, possibly under dangerous conditions, in order to change course.

Weather helm of 3 to 4 degrees is considered desirable, not only from the safety viewpoint but also because it improves the shape of the waterlines. Weather helm acts like the flap on an airplane wing, and tank tests have shown it to be important in providing lift, thus reducing leeway. This small amount of weather helm also gives the helmsman a feel for the boat, which helps him or her do a better job of working the boat up to windward.

The CLP, as a general rule, is calculated using half the rudder area; the CE is calculated using 100% foretriangle area, ignoring the area of overlapping genoas. Fine-lined yachts such as the 6-meter boats have leads of about 6% of the waterline length; average keel cruisers, about 15 to 17%; and beamy, centerboard yachts, perhaps 18 to 20%. Within these ranges the lead will vary depending upon the vessel's characteristics, as follows:

SHORTER LEAD	LONGER LEAD
Fine hull	Beamy hull
Short keel	Long keel
Deep draft	Shoal draft
Fine forward waterlines	Full forward waterlines
Stable vessel	Tender vessel
Low-aspect-ratio rig	High-aspect-ratio rig

If necessary, the lead of any boat can be altered slightly by changing the rake of the mast. Larger changes necessitate moving the mast, recutting the sails, or, if practical, altering the keel or rudder.

CHAPTER SIX

Powering

How Much Power Do You Need?

Having discussed sailing rigs, it is only fair to consider engines. First let's look at engines for sailboats and displacement motorboats.

As a general rule, most American-built sailboats are overpowered. For economical cruising speeds under power, assuming an efficient hull, 3 to 4 brake horsepower per ton of displacement is adequate, 5 b.h.p. per ton is ample, and 6 is often too much. One of my designs, a 40-foot LWL schooner of 48,000 pounds (21.4 tons) displacement, cruises at almost 6 knots with only a 30 b.h.p. engine, a mere 1.4 b.h.p. per ton.

A better guide to engine selection for sailing yachts and displacement powerboats is cubic inches of engine displacement per ton of boat displacement. The accompanying table gives a general recommendation.

Enough reserve power should be available to power engine-run auxiliary devices. Bilge pumps, refrigeration compressors, generators, hydraulic pumps, and other auxiliaries can consume considerable b.h.p. on larger vessels.

Powering planing hulls is different because so much depends on hull shape. Recently, by reshaping

POWER RATING	YACHT TYPE	ENGINE DISPLACEMENT
Light	Bluewater cruisers and ocean racers	5–8 cubic inches per ton
Moderate	Coastal cruisers and light powerboats	8–11 c.i. per ton
Generous	Heavily powered auxiliaries and moderate powerboats	12–15 c.i. per ton
High	Motorsailers and husky displacement cruisers	15–20 c.i. per ton

a modern fiberglass 45-foot production planing yacht from a round-bilge hull to a chine hull, I increased the speed by almost 10% and greatly reduced the stern wave.

The following formula (courtesy of Arthur Edmonds) seems to work well for planing yachts of good hull form:

$$b.h.p = \frac{V^2 \times \text{Displacement (Pounds)}}{28750}$$

Propeller Sizes

For displacement hulls, if efficiency is a prime factor, the reduction gearing should be chosen to turn as large a propeller as possible. For example, the 48,000-pound schooner mentioned previously is geared very low and turns a 25-inch diameter propeller with a 30-b.h.p. engine; thus she performs well with only 1.4 b.h.p. per ton. In auxiliary sailboats, the efficiency of a large propeller must be balanced against the propeller's increased drag under sail. Fortunately, new folding or feathering propellers permit the use of large, efficient two- and even three-bladed props that offer less resistance when the yacht is sailing. The schooner has a variable-pitch propeller; pitch can be adjusted to the load for maximum efficiency when motoring, or lined up fore-and-aft to reduce resistance when sailing.

High-speed craft can efficiently use smaller propellers and do not require the high reduction ratios of the displacement hull. A 2:1 reduction gear is rarely exceeded in semiplaning or planing hulls. Faster small craft often use direct drive, and extremely high-speed boats, such as hydroplanes, use step-up gearing in which propeller r.p.m.s of three times the engine r.p.m.s are common, and a 1500-b.h.p. engine might turn a 14-inch propeller at more than 9000 r.p.m.

In any case, the calculation of propeller size—given a boat's power, speed, hull displacement, etc.—is a complex process beyond the scope of this book. Consult a yacht designer if your boat appears to have problems. You may be pleasantly surprised at the results.

Diesel vs. Gasoline Engines

Diesel engines are now available in sizes from pony to Percheron power and are used in all types of vessels, from small auxiliary cruisers and displacement motorboats to high-speed planing yachts, big oceangoing motoryachts, and commercial vessels of all sizes. Today, gasoline engines are generally found in smaller planing boats and in many beautiful old-timers—both sail and power.

The advantages of diesel engines are fuel safety, greater economy of operation, elimination of periodic tuning of the carburetor and the ignition, and, in most states, a cheaper price per gallon. In fact, the diesel engine offers twice the cruising range per gallon as an equivalent gas engine, and runs on fuel that costs less in many areas. In addition, insurance companies are likely to give better rates for a diesel-powered craft, and the resale value of a diesel-powered vessel is generally higher than that of an equivalent gasoline-powered boat. On the other hand, a diesel engine is heavier and more costly than an equivalent gasoline engine and much more sensitive to fuel cleanliness. A drop of water in the fuel can stop a diesel dead, while the gas engine would barely sputter and keep going.

Gasoline engines are well suited to the light, fast express cruisers in the 20- to 32-foot range, particularly when geared up to a stern drive. Above this size, or in heavier, slower boats, diesel engines are the power plants of choice.

A word of caution from my experience: many diesels are installed improperly. Diesel engines should never be hooked up to galvanized fuel tanks because corrosive elements in the fuel react with the galvanizing and cause it to plug fuel lines. Diesels should not use copper tanks or copper fuel lines either, since gumming can occur. Monel, aluminum, steel, or black-iron tanks with seamless, steel fuel lines are acceptable. Also, diesel exhaust fumes corrode stainless steel exhaust lines in short order.

Single vs. Twin-Screw Powerboats

Powerboat owners are often torn between the choice of single or twin-engine installations. Consider the advantages of each:

Single screw: Economy of first cost
Economy of operation
Simplicity of maintenance
Engine fits lower in hull, occupies less space
Reduced drag of single strut, shaft, and rudder
Prop and rudder are better protected from floating debris

Twin screw: Greater reliability
Better low-speed maneuverability
Engines higher in hull, allow shoaler draft

The reliability of twin screws is often overrated. Usually both engines are drawing fuel from the same tank and, because dirt and water in the fuel is the cause of most engine failures, both engines die within seconds of each other. A wise owner runs the engines off different tanks, through separate fuel filters, and, with luck, avoids a double shutdown. Also, fitting a modern bow thruster (usually a hydraulic motor powering a propeller or jet drive in a tunnel through the bow sections) on a single-screw vessel can do a great deal to offset the twin screw's advantage in maneuverability. Some bow thrusters can swing through a 90-degree arc and act as emergency power if the main engine fails, but these are costly units and may be as expensive as twin screws.

Little thought is given in this country to *wing engines*, but they are popular in Europe. The main power is a single-engine, centerline installation, while the wing engine is smaller, possessing about 25% of the main engine's power. It operates off a separate fuel tank and runs the main shaft through a V-belt and clutch arrangement, or it may have a separate off-center shaft of its own driving a folding or feathering prop. The advantages are the efficiency of a single screw with the reliability of a twin screw, plus the added advantage of an economical small engine for trolling or running auxiliary equipment.

Stern Drives and Outboard Motors

Stern drives, in both single and twin installations, have soared in popularity in the past 20 years and are seen on yachts of all sizes, from open runabouts to large cruisers. The engines may be gas or diesel and can range in power from small 4-cylinder units to V-8s of several hundred horsepower.

They provide excellent power for planing yachts and combine simple installation with excellent steering ability at higher speeds. However, steering problems can arise at low speeds because boats that steer with stern drives do not have a rudder. This can be embarrassing during docking when you throw the engine into neutral and lose all ability to steer in a tricky crosswind or current. Experience in handling this type of power and steering combination is the only remedy. As a rule, someone accustomed to out-

---

FIGURE 6-1

A splash box or well for a transom-mounted outboard helps keep following seas from flooding the boat over the transom cutaway. (From Sea Sense, by Richard Henderson. International Marine, 1991)

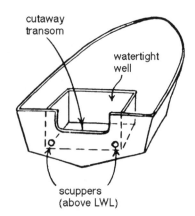

cutaway transom

watertight well

scuppers (above LWL)

board motors has no problems operating a stern drive.

Outboards have their place in smaller power cruisers and as auxiliary power for sailboats. Outboard motors are now available in powers over 200 h.p. We have used one with great success on a husky 30-foot workboat, achieving speeds close to 30 m.p.h. A good friend of mine is now building a 27-foot motorboat of his own design that will be powered to displacement hull speeds by a single 45-h.p. Johnson outboard. I have used an 18-h.p. Evinrude in a heavy 27-foot dory with good results.

The older 2-cycle motors used a gas and oil mix and had rather high fuel consumption, but newer 2-cycle engines meter the oil out of a separate tank and are much cleaner and more efficient. There are also several 4-cycle outboard motors from 6 to 45 h.p. on the market, and these burn straight gasoline.

The outboard motor can now have shaft lengths up to 25 inches. This allows a higher transom and makes for a more seaworthy installation. In any case, the outboard installation needs to be carefully designed to ensure that the relatively low transom cutout drains any waves that come in over the stern.

When used as an auxiliary for a sailboat, the outboard does not have a steering problem since the sailboat's rudder controls the boat when the engine is in neutral. My present boat, a 25-foot, yawl-rigged motorsailer, is powered by a 15-h.p. Honda 4-stroke outboard and performs very efficiently indeed.

CHAPTER SEVEN

Aesthetics

B eauty, as we all know, is in the eye of the beholder. This holds true for yachts as well as for other forms of art. With yachts, however, aesthetic considerations must be balanced with the functional. The good news is that function and beauty are often interconnected. Consider, for example, that the World War II jeep—as practical as a vehicle can get—was chosen as one of the ten most beautiful automobiles of its time by the Museum of Modern Art.

The old standard ratios for sailing yachts follow:

Bow overhang to stern overhang	3:4
Bow angle to stern angle	4:3
LWL to LOA	2:3
Bow freeboard to stern freeboard	8–9:6

Freeboard was the same at the transom as at amidships, with the low point about 80 to 85% of the LWL abaft the bow.

These proportions rarely failed to produce a handsome vessel in the classic style, and may still be used as a guide for judging traditional designs. However, modern sailing yachts will show shorter ends and a proportionately longer waterline to obtain the speed advantage given by the extra length. Such

FIGURE 7-1
Sheerlines. A few of many.

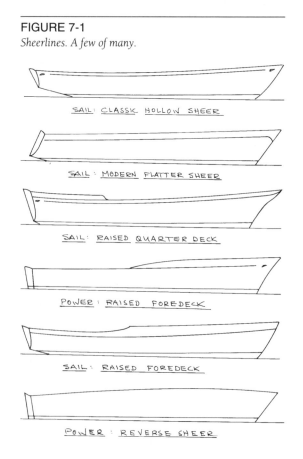

SAIL: CLASSIC HOLLOW SHEER

SAIL: MODERN FLATTER SHEER

SAIL: RAISED QUARTER DECK

POWER: RAISED FOREDECK

SAIL: RAISED FOREDECK

POWER: REVERSE SHEER

craft look best with a considerably flatter sheer than more traditional yachts.

Fast motoryachts today are too often styled to look like seagoing rocket ships, but it seems ridiculous to me to streamline something that rarely goes over 20 to 25 m.p.h. The so-called Italian or Eurostyling with its arbitrary sweeps, stripes, angles, and broken lines is ugly nonsense to my eye, just another fad. If you want to see a proper seagoing fast cruiser, study the work of John Deknatel of Raymond Hunt Associates (Figure 7-2). These are true yachts and will still be handsome when they are 20 years old because they are designed to suit the sea, not a mindless fad. In smaller boats, consider the popular and seaworthy Bartender (Figure 7-3) as an example of a fast vessel designed to a purpose with no exaggeration of style or shape.

Slower powerboats and pure displacement hulls are often styled to resemble tugs or trawlers. This is another fad of the past decade or two. If well done,

such craft may have a timeless appearance that does not grow stale over the years, but all too many are cutesy, cartoon boats. One soon grows weary of looking at them.

Bow Shape

The bows of sailboats take many forms: the spoon, the plumb, the clipper, the raked, and even the tumblehome, as seen on a few catboats. The long spoon bow, now rarely seen except on meter boats, was *de rigueur* on sailing yachts for many years because it reduced the handicap rating yet picked up waterline length and speed as the boat heeled in a press of wind. However, this was only an advantage when the rating rule favored a short waterline; on two boats of the same LOA, a short bow overhang automatically gives a longer LWL and a potentially faster boat.

The shorter LWL of the spoon bow does have the

FIGURE 7-2

This 47-foot semicustom powerboat designed by C. Raymond Hunt Associates and built by Lyman-Morse Shipbuilding of Thomaston, Maine, looks good now and will look good in 20 or 40 years, when Eurostyled powerboats seem like oddities from another era. (C. Raymond Hunt Associates, Inc.)

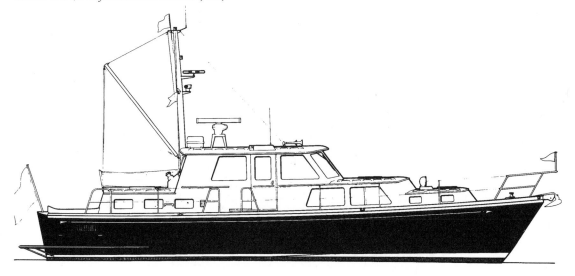

FIGURE 7-3

The Bartender comes in sizes from 19 to 29 feet. She does not look like a rocket ship, but she is very definitely a handsome, seaworthy craft. (George A. Calkins)

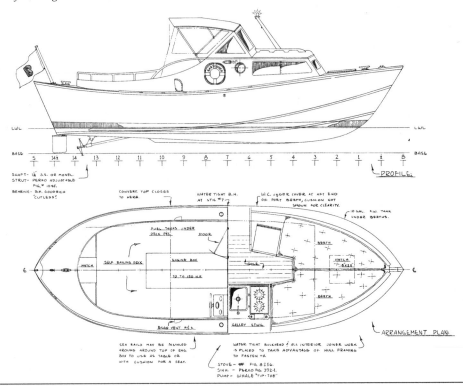

FIGURE 7-4

The Nordhavn 46, a capable world cruiser. (P.A.E. Yacht Builders)

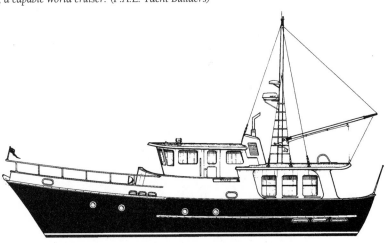

FIGURE 7-5

Bow shapes.

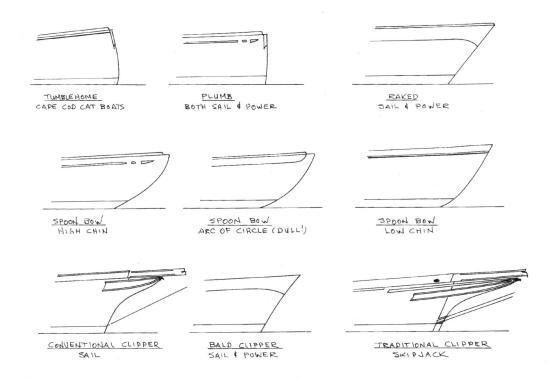

TUMBLEHOME
CAPE COD CAT BOATS

PLUMB
BOTH SAIL & POWER

RAKED
SAIL & POWER

SPOON BOW
HIGH CHIN

SPOON BOW
ARC OF CIRCLE (DULL!)

SPOON BOW
LOW CHIN

CONVENTIONAL CLIPPER
SAIL

BALD CLIPPER
SAIL & POWER

TRADITIONAL CLIPPER
SKIPJACK

advantage of reducing wetted surface when the vessel is running upright or slightly heeled, as opposed to the constant, greater wetted surface of the long waterline, short-stemmed yacht. Of course, modern sailing yachts reduce wetted surface by fin keels and spade rudders, not by spoon bows.

Powerboats in the 1920s and 1930s usually had plumb bows, but this has given way to a semi-clipper bow or, in the Eurostyle, to an exaggerated raked bow. Such shapes provide well-flared forward sections and good reserve buoyancy that combine to assure a drier ride when driving into a choppy sea.

However, these features can be worked into other bow shapes if some thought is given to the design.

Fast boats built of sheet material, plywood in particular, must have reasonably long bow overhangs to provide sufficient flam to the sections for dryness in a seaway at high speeds. Sheet material cannot be bent in two directions at one time, so if the bow is short it must be combined with a narrow deckline or with extremely full chines to fair into a short or plumb stem. These are both undesirable features on planing craft. Displacement powerboats of sheet material are not bothered by finer forward lines because, like a sailboat, they do not punch into a chop at high speed. Still, a flat-sided hull forward is not the best shape for rough water as it may prove wet and miserable in choppy seas. Some bow overhang is desirable to give reasonable flam.

Stern Shape

Stern shapes can vary as widely as bows (Figure 7-6). Today we see transom sterns, counter sterns, reverse transoms, double-enders, inboard rudders, outboard rudders, and other designs. The same advantages and disadvantages that apply to the long spoon bow also apply to the overhanging counter stern. In addition, the reserve buoyancy of the long stern can help prevent pooping when running before the seas and is helpful in obtaining straighter buttock lines. In any case, excess overhangs are to be avoided and are rare on modern yachts.

The reverse transom seen on so many modern sailing yachts has the advantage of reducing weight

FIGURE 7-6
The end! A few of many.

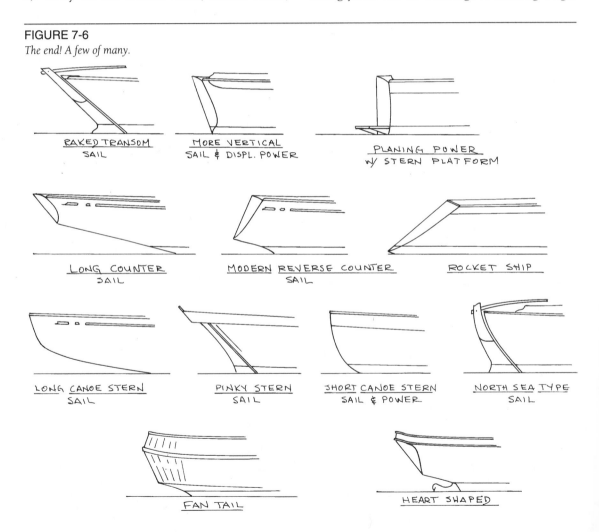

UNDERSTANDING BOAT DESIGN

in the end of the boat, but also reduces the available deck, cockpit, and storage space. Some reverse sterns do provide built-in swim steps and boarding ladders, and buyers have to weigh these features against the disadvantages of lost space.

Lifeboat sterns like those of the North Sea pilot boats are common in bluewater cruisers, but because of the very rounded buttocks they require they almost invariably produce a slow boat and may be prone to pooping due to a lack of reserve buoyancy aft. Their main advantage was specific to their function as workboats. There was no transom corner to be smashed in when the pilot boat pulled away from a freighter in a rough sea, or to foul the net of a fishing boat.

Powerboat sterns are usually of the transom type, although displacement cruisers and fishing craft may use double-ended hulls. Some of the Eurostyled craft appear to have a reverse transom, but usually this is just a styling feature that extends past a true transom stern and may support a swim platform. A true reverse transom on a motoryacht scoops up water when going astern and does not make a great deal of sense.

Cabin Shape

Deck structures play a large part in the appearance of a vessel and must be given considerable thought if they are to harmonize with the hull. The cabin should have a flatter curve than the sheerline. Usually it is much flatter, and on some designs may be a straight line. As a rule, the roof edge should parallel the LWL or increase in height as it runs aft, but it rarely looks good if lower aft than forward.

The cabin sides must lean inboard slightly (tumblehome) or they will appear to be falling outboard; ¼ inch of tumblehome per foot of height is a good minimum ratio, although modern craft, both power and sail, may have much more. Heavy streamlining

and rounding of the corners can look good, but may result in an unnecessarily costly structure when done in wood or metal. In fiberglass craft, such rounding adds to strength and avoids weak, sharp, easily chipped corners. Still, rounding should not be excessive or the deckhouse will resemble an inverted bathtub.

Most modern powerboats, motorsailers, and a few auxiliaries have very large windows. Although this results in a bright, airy interior, it can also let in too much sunlight on hot days and too much water in heavy weather. Large powerboat windows—especially sliding or drop-sash varieties—are rarely watertight. The strongest and tightest of the opening windows are those with aluminum frames and hinged glass. In any case, a boat with large expanses of glass should have strong storm shutters of aluminum, plywood, or plastic if it is to be taken offshore. Lexan makes excellent shutters since it is both strong and translucent.

Small craft and vessels of low stability or shoal hulls should not be fitted with high deckhouses in an attempt to gain standing headroom. Sitting headroom is quite ample for small boats in any case. How much walking can you do in a cabin 8 feet long with a sole 2 feet wide? The high house raises the center of

Pastime is a motor yacht with timeless styling. She will still be handsome 50 years from now. The 48-footer was designed by Spencer Lincoln and built by Lyman-Morse in Thomaston, Maine.

gravity, thus reducing stability and increasing windage.

The rake of cabin houses, windows, stanchions, and other topside structures should change gradually, if at all. In too many designs the shape and rake of windows, bridges, and other structures have no relation to the main house or to each other. This is particularly true with the Eurostyled jetships. It results in a hodgepodge of angles. Such boats remind me of a Dali painting.

Finally, bear in mind that function is beauty. Phony exhaust ports, unnecessary stripes, fluting, and nonfunctional trim have no place on a yacht— whether power or sail. I believe, in the future, that many contemporary yachts will look as phony as a 1960 Cadillac, with its tailfins and garish chrome, does today.

Houseboats

Once, houseboats were charming little shanties with flowerpots and auto-tire fenders on barge-like hulls. Today, they are gleaming fiberglass speedsters capable of pulling half a dozen water skiers and accommodating a family in style. Once the haven of the low-rent set, modern houseboats are comfortable, powerful, fast, and streamlined. Their numbers are growing so quickly that a few seaside towns, fearing they may become, like Hong Kong, a home for hundreds of non-taxpaying residents, have legislated against live-aboards.

The hull of the slow, rough-riding shanty boat was simply a barge, or perhaps a couple of pontoons, on which the box-like superstructure was set. The hull was deliberately shoal, so it could be run up on a sandbar for the night and used in many thousands of miles of knee-deep waterways. Newer houseboat hulls are more sophisticated, with proper flare and shape forward, and can give a decent ride in a chop if not driven too hard. But even with these improvements they still perform best at slow speeds in protected waters.

The wide expanse of deck space, the roomy interior, and the stable life of a houseboat can provide many hours of breezy relaxation afloat, but these boats are not safe offshore, where you might be caught by strong winds, high seas, and adverse tides. Low freeboard, large windows, high cabin sides, great windage, and a shallow hull do not combine to create a seaworthy vessel. Houseboats are more at home on rivers, canals, and well-protected bays.

The scow and the garvey hull types are excellent choices for an amateur-built houseboat intended for moderate speeds. The boat can be built of sheet material and poses few problems to a competent carpenter. Such hulls are usually of plywood, although steel or aluminum is equally feasible, and go together quickly and easily compared with more complex hulls.

Character Boat

Many yachtsmen prefer the romance and beauty of bygone days to the cool efficiency of the modern auxiliary sailboat or motoryacht. For this reason, our waters are still dotted with many interesting and appealing vessels—originals and replicas of such models as Friendship sloops, Cape Cod cats, sharpies, pinkies, bugeyes, skipjacks, Block Island cowhorns, coasting schooners, and a host of other working types. Powerboat men and women yearn for small editions of tugs, trawlers, and rumrunners, while many still enjoy the silence and fascination of steam launches. Still, there are certain drawbacks to true, antique character boats that should be understood before the dreamer takes a step he may regret.

First, you should know that many working boats were designed to be inexpensive and functional. Fishing boats, for example, often require inexpensive construction, including flat frames, galvanized fastenings, and inside ballast. They also require low freeboard for ease of hauling nets and traps, and other features that may make the vessel unsuitable for yachting. The accommodations are tight by present standards, with cramped headroom and few of the facilities expected on most yachts. On older boats, the engine and tank installations may be unsafe and the ventilation inadequate. If you can live with these drawbacks and afford to correct them where necessary, then have the vessel surveyed by an expert in order to disclose any serious faults before taking the plunge.

Performance is another area of concern. Inside ballast, gaff rigs, long keels, shoal draft, slack rigging, and rough, unfair hulls are not conducive to speed or weatherliness under sail. The older, narrower powerboat styles may roll you inside out in a beam sea. In addition, older boats require a great deal of maintenance, and, even then, they are rarely tight, dry hulls. Fishermen didn't mind pumping a few strokes every hour, and, since they rarely slept aboard, leaky decks and soggy blankets were not a big worry.

Modern replicas and newly designed character boats do not have the ills of construction, age, and condition that beset the original craft. They often perform better too, due to major improvements in hull shape, newer and smoother hulls, better balance of hull and rig, and improved machinery. In many cases, sailing character boats of new design have completely modern hulls and rigs, with fin keels and tall Bermudan rigs. The only concessions to character are in the clipper bow, trailboards, and styling. Such craft perform right along with their contemporary sisters and hardly merit the term "character boat." Indeed, they are built of modern epoxy and wood construction, fiberglass, aluminum, or even more exotic materials that would have an old salt turning in his grave with envy.

Character powerboats today are rarely original fishing craft; if they are in good shape, they are still fishing. One class of working boats that has been lovingly restored is the tug, and many of them now operate as yachts, at least in the Northwest. Many older yachts, both cruisers and runabouts, of the 1920s and 1930s are still afloat as well, and still meticulously cared for by proud owners. If you are interested in our wonderful heritage of antique wooden craft, you must attend some of the wooden boat shows held annually throughout the United States and Canada.

Newly built character powerboats are, too often, fiberglass, V-bottom semidisplacement hulls with pretty sheerlines and somewhat squared off upper works. The Grand Banks line is typical of the so-called trawler yachts that come out of the Far East by the thousands. While many of these yachts are handsome and practical in their own right, they bear about as much resemblance to a true trawler as my Ford van bears to a Mack truck. Their speed is lower than an out-and-out planing hull, but this is compensated for by comfort and economy. The same hull could be given a straight sheerline and modern, streamlined styling with no change in seaworthiness or performance, but then it would not be a character boat to anyone's way of thinking.

CHAPTER EIGHT

The Accommodation Layout

Sleeping Space

Most small boats, power or sail, have too many berths and too little storage space. It is ridiculous to expect to cruise six people in a 25-footer and not have them be babbling idiots inside of a week. The usual excuse for having too many berths on racing sailboats is that the bunks are necessary for a large crew. Baloney! If it is really a racing yacht, the berths are full of sails most of the time and the crew sleeps "hot bunk" (the crewman coming off watch jumps into the hot bunk just vacated by his replacement). Once the race is over, everyone heads for the nearest hotel. If many boats had fewer berths and more sail stowage, they would be better for both racing and cruising. The problem is to convince the buyer of this.

Comfortable racing-sailboat berths should be fairly narrow. It sounds crazy, but you bash around too much in a wide berth in any kind of a seaway. Widths of 22 inches are fine, and 24 to 26 inches is ample. Of course, adequate leeboards are essential on sailing craft to keep the crew in the berth, instead of on the cabin sole. These should be about 10 inches high. Dacron leecloths are best, tied off to padeyes in the overhead. Powerboat berths can be 30 inches wide, but a leeboard or cloth is still desirable if the boat goes offshore. Sleeping in a steep beam sea is impossible if you are always afraid of being thrown out of your berth.

Berth cushions of foam plastic make sense because they do not develop the smells of foam rubber. Four-inch thickness is a reasonable minimum, and six inches is better. Thinner mattresses can be used if the berth bottom is cloth, Dacron, or canvas instead of plywood. The weight savings of the cloth bottom and the thinner mattress is significant on a racing yacht.

If upper berths are fitted, they should be 22 inches or more above the lower berths. An aluminum pipe frame with a Dacron bottom laced in and a two-inch mattress makes an excellent upper berth. The design should allow the upper berth to be leveled when the boat heels. This gives a great deal of extra comfort, provided the skipper doesn't decide to tack while you are sound asleep. Leecloths are still required, of course.

Double berths are popular today and are quite suitable for powerboats and for cruising yachts that rarely go to sea, spending most of their nights in har-

FIGURE 8-1

(1) Bob Wallstrom's one-cabin plan for the 26-foot Lubec Boat succeeds by not attempting to cram too much accommodation into a small place. Essentially a two-person boat, the berths double as settee; the dining table tilts up out of the way when not in use. No attempt was made to give the toilet its own enclosure, which would have taken a lot more space than shown. The galley and hanging lockers are aft, eliminating the possibility of quarter berths. (2) Bill Luders's Sea Sprite 30 is representative of the typical aft cockpit layout: V-berths forward, settees in the saloon, and aft galley. A formal dinette would have severely restricted traffic flow; the fold-down bulkhead-mounted table is a satisfactory solution. (3) The McMurdy & Rhodes Hinckley Sou'Wester 51 has a voluminous interior divided by a center cockpit. Three private staterooms are featured as well as two heads, large galley and dinette, and generous stowage compartments. (From Yacht Style, by Dan Spurr. International Marine, 1990)

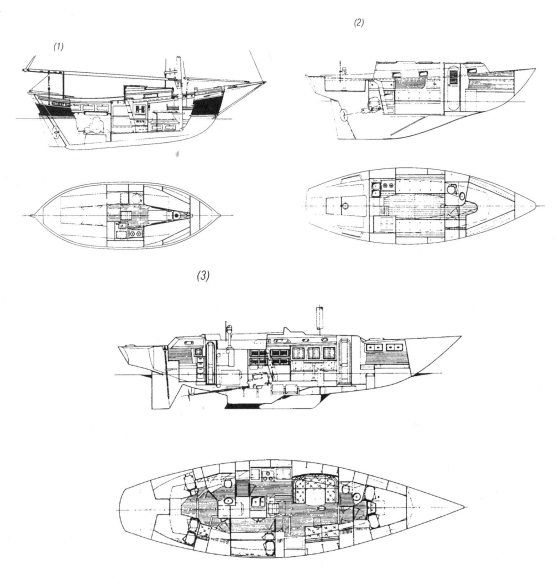

(2)

(1)

(3)

THE ACCOMMODATION LAYOUT

bor. If the boat is used offshore a great deal, the mattress should be split down the center and a Dacron leeboard fitted to keep the sleepers apart when the boat is rolling in beam seas or sailing along at a good angle of heel.

Powerboats may use dinettes and convertible dinettes which form a double berth to good advantage. However, I do not favor a dinette on a sailboat as it is impossible to sit comfortably in the athwartship seat when the boat is rolling or heeled over. U-shaped dinettes do provide some useful seating when the boat is heeled, but I favor the old drop-leaf table between two fore-and-aft settee berths for the average sailing yacht of medium size. Like dinettes, athwartship berths should be avoided on offshore craft because they are uncomfortable in a rolling beam sea.

Galley Gear

The galley should be set up so the cook can provide hearty meals in any weather. On a small boat in rough going, this may be just soup and a sandwich, while on a large yacht it may mean a gourmet meal if the cook and the crew's stomachs are up to it.

On boats with standing headroom the galley top should be 36 to 37 inches above the sole, and if the boat has only sitting headroom the galley top should

be about 12 inches higher than the seat. In any case, the working space must be provided with high *fiddles* (sea rails) to keep things in place in a rough sea; this applies to both sail and powerboats. The fiddles should be about 1¼ to 1½ inches high and open for a few inches at the corners to facilitate cleaning. They should also be strongly bolted in place to serve as emergency handholds.

The choice of stove fuel is a matter of personal preference. Propane is the most popular choice for powerboats and larger sailing yachts, despite the danger of explosion. It is handy and burns hot, but the installation is fairly costly and can be dangerous if not done properly. The tanks must be installed in a well-ventilated space where any spillage will drain overboard. A solenoid switch that turns off the valve at the tank when the stove is not in use should be fitted. Propane is readily available and not expensive.

I prefer alcohol fuel. It is nonexplosive, so a fiery spill can be easily extinguished with water. Modern alcohol stoves, such as the Swedish Origo, are not pressurized and cannot flare up; they are safe, pleasant to use, and surprisingly fast. We even baked ribs in the oven-fitted Origo on our last boat. Alcohol fuel is not cheap (about $9 per gallon), but two or three gallons seems to last us all season—not an unbearable expense.

All boat stoves should have high sea rails to keep the pots in place in a seaway, and sailboat stoves

FIGURE 8-2 (opposite)

(1) The Nordhavn 46 long-range cruiser has a guest stateroom forward with a head in the forepeak, owner's stateroom amidships under the wheelhouse, and saloon with dinette, swivel seats, and adjacent galley. Access to the wheelhouse is by stairs either from the saloon or passageway outside the staterooms. (2) Though the forward V-sections of most high-performance sportboats are a limiting factor, the accommodations of the 60-footer built by the famous Italian firm of Cantieri Navali Di Baia are more than ample, thanks in part to a beam of almost 18 feet. As is common in this type of yacht, much space is given to conversational seating and lounging areas. (3) The Blue Seas 31 is a Down East "lobster yacht" with dual steering stations. The flared bow narrows sharply at the water, compressing the V-berths. The saloon has a settee that can be converted to a guest berth, but otherwise there is little room for visitors; the cockpit is a trade-off against increased accommodation. (4) Several floor plans are possible in Ocean Yachts' 53-foot motoryacht. Two decks dramatically increase the designer's options. The plan shown has a guest stateroom forward, owner's stateroom aft, and a third abaft the engine room. The galley, saloon, and several seating areas are situated on the main deck. (From Yacht Style, *by Dan Spurr. International Marine, 1990)*

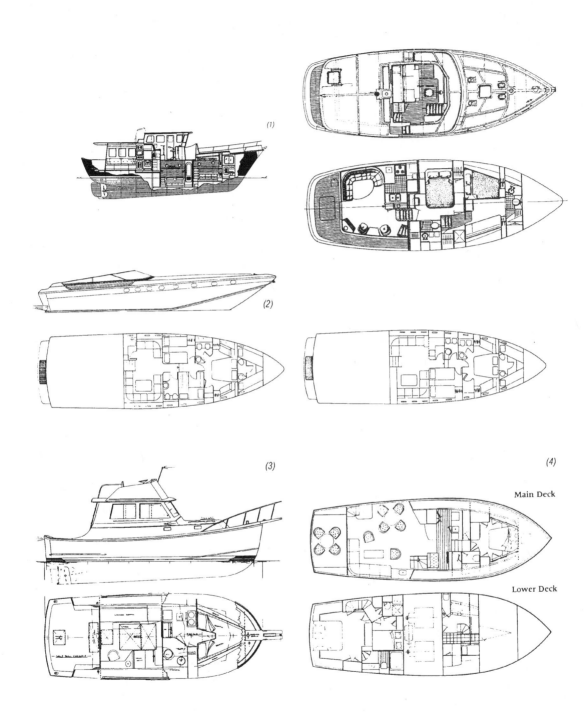

(1)

(2)

(3)

(4)

Main Deck

Lower Deck

THE ACCOMMODATION LAYOUT

should be gimbaled if possible to prevent scalding spills. On powerboats and on sailboats with non-gimbaled stoves, it is safer to place the stove so the cook stands or sits forward or aft of the stove and not inboard of it. Then, if a pot spills due to the vessel's roll, the cook is less likely to be burned. The cook should never stand inboard of a fixed stove, even in a calm harbor, because the wake from a passing boat could flip a pot, with disastrous results.

Large boats may use diesel stoves, or even electric stoves if they have a big auxiliary generator. Gasoline stoves, like the popular Coleman models, are too dangerous to have aboard, and solid fuel stoves, such as Sterno, are too slow to be useful except as a spare burner in a pinch.

Top-opening iceboxes are best because less cold air is lost when the box is opened, and because food does not spill out when the vessel is rolling in a beam sea or sailing at a steep angle of heel. Small boats can make good use of a large portable ice chest. We have two of them on our *Phialle*. With built-in iceboxes the lining should be monel, stainless steel, or fiberglass for ease of cleaning, and the insulation at least 3 inches thick all around. Indeed, 4 inches of insulation on the sides and even more on the bottom is better. The box should drain to a bottle that can be emptied overboard, or it can have a pump to drain it into the sink. It should never be drained into the bilge. Besides the inevitable smell, in a wooden boat water in the bilge can cause rot. Electric refrigeration is feasible on larger craft. I prefer to have the refrigeration run off the 12- or 24-volt ship's power, rather than 110 VAC: otherwise you cannot leave the boat for long unless you are plugged into a dock outlet. Running refrigeration off the same voltage as the ship's power does require a large battery bank and a husky alternator.

Sinks should be deep, 9 to 10 inches, and of good size. Some small production boats use shallow, round basins, but they are really quite useless. If a pressure water system is fitted, a backup manual pump is a must. I like to see this pump fitted with a tee so it can draw seawater when not needed for freshwater backup. Foot pumps are handier than hand pumps because you can run water and use both hands to wash the dishes.

Plumbing

The W.C. (water closet) is a problem these days due to modern antipollution laws. In very small craft, 20 feet or less, the old cedar bucket may be the only answer. However, most small cruisers have space under a seat or V berth for a decent porta-potti. There are a few good ones on the market. The cost is minimal, and the operation is simple, although emptying the porta-potti is unpleasant. Where space permits, it is best to have the W.C. lined up fore-and-aft because it allows the user to brace against the roll of the boat. This is especially helpful on sailboats, where it is difficult to use a toilet when the boat is heeling 20 degrees or more.

Larger craft have proper marine toilets, which, if legal, are hooked up to holding tanks that store the effluent until it can be pumped out. Pumping can be done at shore stations or, if the boat has the proper valving, when the boat is more than three miles offshore. In the latter case, ensure there is a lock to keep the valve in the holding tank position when you are sailing inshore waters, or you may receive a citation. Some areas do not allow Y valves (Lake Champlain, the Great Lakes, and others), so check local regulations. On larger boats with good battery power an electrically operated waste-treatment unit (e.g., Electro-San) may be fitted, but, again, this is illegal in certain waters so check first before you invest in a costly installation.

Showers are becoming standard equipment on smaller and smaller boats every year. Since they consume a great deal of water, a workable arrangement is a saltwater tap for showering and a freshwater tap for rinsing. This is not practical in northern waters, though, as the first sting of icy seawater may send a naked bather howling into the saloon. The shower should drain into a fiberglass or metal tray, from which it is then pumped overboard. Like the icebox, the shower should never drain into the bilges. This is done on some boats, resulting in very unpleasant odors.

It should be borne in mind that there is serious talk of closing some waters to all discharges. This means that even shower and galley sink water may have to be collected in a holding tank and pumped ashore. It seems unreasonable to me, and if it becomes law it will create problems for many small-boat owners. How big a tank will we need for a long cruise?

Hot water for the galley and heads is best provided by a kind of heat exchanger that operates off the engine waste water and holds 8 to 10 gallons of fresh water. These units can keep water hot for a day or so, but only work with freshwater-cooled inboard motors because seawater-cooled engines do not build up enough heat in the exhaust water. Bear in mind, too, that a modern diesel engine runs at temperatures of 170 to 180 degrees. The water in these tanks can be scalding and must be mixed with cold water. This is particularly important to remember when you have children aboard. Many of the marine hot-water heaters also operate off 110 VAC and can be used at dockside without running the engine.

Storage

Storage space on small boats should be given more consideration than it usually gets. Too often, one tiny hanging locker is provided along with a few drawers and bins. The rest of the space is taken up

with unneeded berths. List the gear that you must store aboard your next boat, and you will see why ample stowage space is essential. Shelves, bins, or lockers should be provided for all of the following gear: charts, navigating instruments, food, dishes, cutlery, cooking utensils, cleaning supplies, garbage, clothing, dirty laundry, towels, bedding, fenders, mooring and dock lines, spare lines, fishing gear, crab traps, spare parts, tools, foul-weather gear, extra sails, life jackets, and so on. Also desirable are racks for binoculars, flashlights, a hand-bearing compass, and other items that must be close at hand.

In larger craft, it is helpful to have a separate small drawer in the heads where each crew member can store his personal toiletries. A separate drawer for each crew member's clothing is also desirable if space permits. On a very large yacht it is a fine idea to have a luggage locker where guests' empty suitcases (they shouldn't, but they will, bring them) can be stored.

Anchor-line stowage is almost always in the fore-peak, but on many boats it is allowed to fall into a shapeless bundle at the bottom of the forepeak where it slowly mildews. This is not too serious with fiber-glass boats and nylon lines, but wooden boats should have a grating to support the line so it can dry out. Otherwise there is danger of mildew and eventual rot from the damp line. A good ventilator reduces problems in this area.

Ventilation

Ventilation is seldom given the attention it deserves in power craft. Sailboats of any size usually have two *dorade vents* (large cowl ventilators mounted on water-trap boxes, which let fresh air below while steering the rain and spray overboard), and larger auxiliaries may have four, six, or more dorades ventilating all parts of the yacht. In contrast, power craft up to 40 feet and larger rarely have

FIGURE 8-3

Because there are few square shapes inside a boat, furniture foundations and stowage compartments assume some peculiar geometric shapes. The fine entry lines of both sailboats and powerboats are particularly challenging to naval architects, and oftentimes unfathomable to the untrained eye. The space that appears to be generous in the accommodation or floor plan may not be there at all when viewed in cross section. Notice how the V and round shapes of these hulls produce oddly shaped lockers and berths. (From Yacht Style, by Dan Spurr. International Marine, 1990)

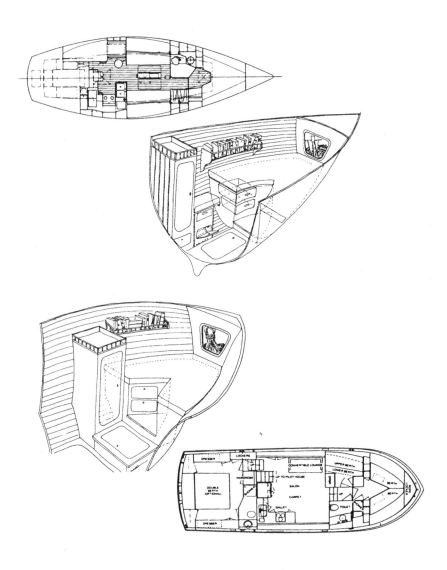

proper vents and usually depend on their large opening windows or ports for ventilation. This is fine in good weather when the crew is aboard to open the windows, but it is not worth much in rainy weather or when the boat is locked up at the dock during the week.

Both power and sail boats can make use of the new solar-powered "flying saucer" vents produced by Nicro Fico and others. There are also cowl vents with built-in rain and spray guards that can be very useful on all boats.

Adequate ventilation goes a long way toward eliminating musty odors and mildew, which can creep in when the boat is left unused for any length of time.

Furnishings

A boat should not resemble a floating palace. Bear in mind: anything that can be scratched, chipped, stained, waterlogged, knocked over, fallen against, or damaged in any way, will be. If you furnish accordingly, you will have a much happier ship.

Plain painted furniture with natural trim to suit is easy to maintain. Galley, table, and locker tops of Formica are excellent if you remember that such surfaces are very slippery, and that items placed on them have a life of their own in any kind of a sea. Bulkheads and other large surfaces can also be Formica covered to reduce maintenance. Carpeting should not shrink if wet and should be easily removable for drying if it gets damp, or it may develop musty odors. A high quality indoor-outdoor carpet is a good choice. Otherwise, cabin soles should be teak or painted wood.

Deep fiddles are essential on all locker tops, tables, and shelves in order to keep things in place. They should be 2 inches high. Fiddles are rarely seen on dinette tables in small craft because the table top doubles as a berth bottom. A wise owner has removeable fiddles fitted. Drawers should have a strong, positive catch or be designed to lift ¼ inch to open. Locker doors should also be fitted with positive catches or turn-buttons. The magnetic catches seen on many small craft are not practical because they are too weak to hold heavy items in a seaway and are prone to rust. Hardware of solid brass, bronze, or stainless steel is the only type suitable for vessels. Plated steel, Zamac, or similar junk does not last.

Cushions and mattresses covered with Naugahyde stay dry until someone sleeps on them; then they get wet, sticky, and uncomfortable. They are a real misery in warm weather. Terry-cloth or sailcloth covers are more comfortable to sleep on and dry easily if they do get wet. They can also be removed easily for cleaning if they are made with large zippers. The zippers should be nylon or brass, never steel, for obvious reasons. Fancy fabrics such as velours, silks, and velvets have no place on a yacht, where they are subjected to salt water, spilled coffee—what have you. Leave them in your drawing room.

CHAPTER NINE

Safety at Sea

S afety in small boats boils down to a few basics: keep the crew aboard and safe when below, keep the water out, understand fire prevention, and be prepared and equipped to fight fires.

Safety On Deck

Safety on deck begins with keeping the crew aboard, and this requires adequately wide side decks. On some designs the side decks are so narrow that the crew must perform a tightrope act to get forward. Solid handrails, through-bolted to the roof or cabin sides and not simply screwed in place, are essential. Toerails help to keep your feet from slipping overboard on wet decks. Nonskid paint or varnish, or bare teak decking, is also necessary. Too many powerboats have dangerously slick decks and cabin roofs and often they compound the problem by having inadequate toerails and slippery, stainless steel handrails.

Bow pulpits and rails are of great assistance when handling sails or anchors on the foredeck. Heights of 24 inches, although common, are too low and may

actually catch you behind the knees and contribute to flipping you overboard. For safety, 28 to 30 inches high is desirable, but there should be an intermediate lifeline at half the height for the safety of children and of adults who might otherwise be washed overside while lying on deck. Lifelines of plastic-covered wire supported by husky stanchions are required equipment on offshore racing yachts and are seen on most sailing cruisers as well. They should be installed on powerboats more often than they are. All rails and stanchions must be through-bolted for safety, and not simply screwed in place.

Crew members should be provided with safety harnesses that can be clipped to the lifelines or rigging, thus freeing both hands for work if necessary. Still, the old rule, "One hand for yourself and one for the ship," is a good one to live by whenever possible. The oceangoing vessel must also be equipped with life jackets fitted with lights, dye markers, and drogues. A very complete list of gear is required on all well-supervised distance races, and it is a rare (read disqualified) yacht that is deficient in this respect. Cruising men and women should make note of the racing yacht's inventory of safety gear.

As well as keeping the crew aboard, the wise

skipper practices man-overboard drills and is pre-pared for emergencies. The Life Sling, developed in the Northwest, is a very useful piece of equipment for getting a crewman back aboard. Videotapes demonstrating its use are available at many marine chandleries.

Safety Below

Below decks it is necessary to have adequate handrails, leeboards, and safety straps so that crew members are not injured in a fall. Fore-and-aft handrails should be through-bolted to the cabin overhead—one on the centerline in small craft, and two rails a few feet apart in larger vessels. Strong fiddles, through-bolted, can act as handrails in an emergency as well. We have mentioned leeboards on the berths, but a seldom-seen and very useful safety feature is a waist-high handrail within easy reach of the toilet.

The galley should be fitted with a rail so the cook cannot fall into the stove. A waist belt, or straps, add security since the cook often needs both hands to work. Also, a safe skipper insists that the cook wear foul-weather gear if the sea is rough, since this can prevent bad burns in case of a scalding spill.

Keeping Water Out

The windows and ports of offshore cruisers should have adequate shutters that can be bolted in place in an emergency. Hatches require covers, shutters, or other means of closing off the large area in an emergency, and ventilators need plugs or other means to close off the opening. Seacocks must be fitted on all through-hull openings. They should be seated on heavy reinforcement, be kept in good working order, and have a soft pine plug nearby in case the seacock

or hose fails. The hose to the seacock should be fastened with two stainless steel hose clamps.

Fuel fills and tank vents need attention on the bluewater cruiser as well. I once spent seven days getting to Bermuda because salt water had entered the fuel-tank vents, knocked out the engine with its attendant electrical supply, and left us dependent on wind and sun sights (in cloudy weather) to complete the trip. The deck fills can have their threads coated with waterproof grease (but only if there is a can of waterproof grease aboard), and the vents can be fitted with covers or sealed off with plastic food wrap in an emergency. Since powerboats must have their fuel-tank vents open, careful installation is essential to ensure they are out of reach of the seas and protected from rain and spray.

Self-bailing cockpits are now fitted to almost all sailing yachts except the very smallest. The companionway door should be able to be blocked up to the height of the cockpit seats, with removable slides if a permanent bridge deck is not fitted, so water does not rush below before it can drain. In the event it takes on water, the cockpit should be small enough that the weight of the water does not trim down the stern so far that seas climb aboard faster than the drains it them out. Overly large cockpits can be filled in as necessary with Styrofoam blocking, firmly held in place.

If it does enter, water must be pumped out as quickly as possible. An adequate hand pump is essential, no matter how many electric or engine-operated pumps are aboard, and it must be one that can suck trash without clogging. Although it has been said that the best pump is a frightened man with a bucket, I like the big diaphragm pumps, like those made by Edson in the United States and Whale and Henderson in England. These pumps should be mounted so they can be operated from the helm in case the skipper is alone. A second pump, operable from below decks, is advisable on larger craft.

Fire Protection

Safety at sea also involves precautions against fire. Adequate fire extinguishers are required by the regulations of the U.S. Coast Guard. A little overkill in this department makes good sense. The installation of fuel tanks and lines, stoves, gas bottles, and other potential fire hazards must receive attention as well. This book cannot hope to cover all facets of these installations, and the concerned yachtsman is referred to *Standards and Recommended Practices for Small Craft*. This publication is available from the American Boat and Yacht Council (P.O. Box 747, 405 Headquarters Drive, Suite 3, Millersville, MD 21108) and covers the installation of L.P.G. systems, stoves, fire extinguishers, electrical systems, engine, fuel tanks, engine-room ventilation, and many other safety devices afloat. Manual NFPA 302, *Fire Protection Standard for Pleasure and Commercial Motor Craft*, put out by the National Fire Protection Association (Batterymarch Park, Quincy, MA 02269), also contains a wealth of information.

It is interesting that yachts built under Lloyds' survey and classified 100A must be surveyed at regular intervals, and have a special rigorous survey at longer intervals, in order to retain the 100A rating. The purpose of the surveys is to ensure that the yacht and its equipment are in seaworthy condition. Any vessel that is in poor condition, or is not repaired as required by the survey, is dropped from classification immediately. Owners of other vessels would do well to follow this practice. If boats were inspected by a competent marine surveyor every two or three years, they could be kept in safe condition, and defects could be corrected before they required major repairs or resulted in the loss of the ship or its crew. The owner can perform his or her own less rigorous survey using the U.S. Coast Guard Auxiliary's examination as set forth in the Appendices.

CHAPTER TEN

Construction

Boatbuilding is a vast subject. Obviously, we cannot explain and detail the wide range of boat construction methods. Instead, this chapter is meant to point out some of the desirable features of the main materials: wood, fiberglass, steel, and aluminum.

Wood

Wood yachts and workboats, built a number of ways, can last for many years with reasonable care. As one of the judges of the Victoria Classic Boat Show, I have seen many wooden boats that are still in fine, seaworthy condition after 40, 60, and 100 years of service. A big advantage of traditional wood construction is that the boat is formed, basically, from a bundle of planks or timbers that are glued, nailed, or screwed together. This may create problems, but it also means that any part of the vessel that deteriorates can be individually replaced and the craft made as good as new. Sometimes the repair only requires the replacement of one or two planks or frames. Sometimes it may mean extensive reconstruction, but it can usually be done at a reasonable price, and the work is not beyond the skill of a competent amateur craftsman.

Wood Planking

Lapstrake, also called *clinker* or *clencher*, is an old form of wood construction, dating back to Viking times. The plank seams are overlapped and fastened with rivets, bolts, or screws. To be watertight, lapstrake hulls depend on a snug fit and the swelling of the wood. Problems can develop with this type of construction, particularly in riveted hulls, when the fasteners stretch, the wood shrinks, and the vessel begins to leak. Refastening is the only answer because caulking only forces the seams farther apart. The advantage of lapstrake hulls is that thinner planking may be used due to the doubling at every seam, and this can produce a light hull. In powerboats the laps tend to throw off the spray and make for a dry boat. Lapstrake sailing craft are at a disadvantage, however, because the laps create extra wetted surface and slow the boat in light breezes.

Lapstrake hulls have been built of marine-grade plywood planks with good results. The plywood shrinks and swells less than standard planking, so

FIGURE 10-1

Planking methods.

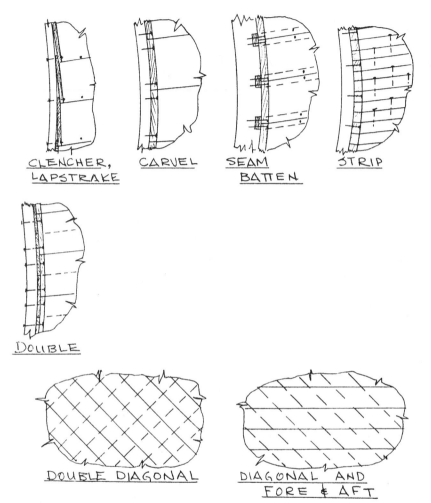

CLENCHER, LAPSTRAKE

CARVEL

SEAM BATTEN

STRIP

DOUBLE

DOUBLE DIAGONAL

DIAGONAL AND FORE & AFT

some of the problems are reduced.

Carvel (often erroneously called smooth skin) may be built using a number of different systems: regular planking, seam-batten planking, strip planking, edge-glued planking, double planking, double-diagonal planking, laminated planking, and others. Traditional carvel planking requires closely spaced frames.

To make the seams watertight, a caulking of cotton strands is driven between the planks with a caulking iron. Light racers may have tightly fitted planking with the edges glued instead of caulked. This method demands first-class workmanship and maintenance and, as a result, is rarely used on cruising yachts.

Strip planking is ideal for the amateur craftsman.

The plank strips are usually square, about as narrow as they are thick, and are glued and edge-nailed together to form a solid hull. This results in a tight, strong, low-maintenance vessel. The narrow strips are easily handled and fitted without the need for the fine craftsmanship that is required of glued-seam construction with wider planking. By using planking that is thicker than normal, the frames in the boat can be widely spaced or eliminated altogether if the vessel's bulkheads are used to provide athwartship strength.

Seam-batten planking is another method that requires no caulking, because the planks are glued and fastened to longitudinal battens at each plank seam. The battens ensure a watertight seam and also reinforce the planking so that thinner planking can be used with resultant weight savings. Seam-batten planking requires sawn frames, which can be notched to hold the battens. For this reason, the method is favored in chine powerboats because they normally employ sawn frames, and because the light-weight nature of seam-batten boats benefits planing performance.

Double planking and double-diagonal planking are similar. Both obtain a watertight seam from glue-ing (generally with a gap-filling epoxy today) the outer layer of planking to the inner layer. Older craft may have light canvas soaked in glue or varnish or white lead between the layers, but the cloth can rot in time, creating serious problems. Double planking usually has both plank layers running fore-and-aft, although the inner layer could run diagonally. Multi-layer systems, often called cold molded, use thinner planks glued up in three to ten layers and all set in epoxy to produce a one-piece, seamless hull. These are tight, strong craft and may be built with few or no frames if the plank thickness is sufficient. Multilayer vessels with a number of diagonal inner layers are often built over closely spaced longitudinal framing for strength and lightness.

Older cold-molded hulls, built before the advent of modern resorcinol and epoxy glues, can have problems of delamination. They must be carefully surveyed before being purchased. A few hulls, in sizes up to 40 feet, were built by Luders Marine in a hot-molded process using mahogany veneers, resorcinol glue, and vacuum bags to obtain gluing pressure. These boats have held up well and many are still sailing 30 to 40 years after their launching. Due to the high cost of labor, this method has been replaced by fiberglass construction for modern production yachts.

Laminated hulls can be difficult to repair if the planking is holed, particularly if they are built frame-less and have nothing to attach the replacement planking to. This is a job for experts and may require a fiberglass patch inside the hull.

Wood Hull Framing

The framing of wood hulls can take almost as many different forms as the planking. Steam-bent, sawn, double-sawn, longitudinal, bulkhead, and laminated frames or composite construction are the most common forms.

Closely spaced steam-bent frames are commonly seen in round-bilged powerboats and in sailing craft up to medium size. A proper steam-bent frame is square or nearly square in cross section to provide good athwartship strength and a solid base for the fastenings. Some low-quality craft have thin, wide frames that are easier to bend than square frames. These frames are fitted on the flat, and the planking is fastened with rivets or galvanized clench nails. They have little transverse strength and are prone to splitting and to breaking at hard curves; in short, they are not good construction.

Sawn frames are cut out of solid wood to the required shape. They may be made in several pieces in order to get around the curves of the hull, in

FIGURE 10-2
Framing methods.

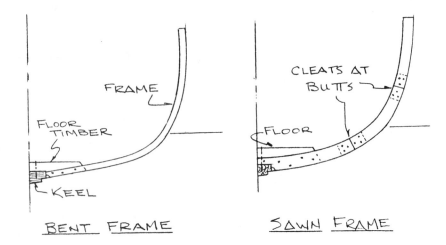

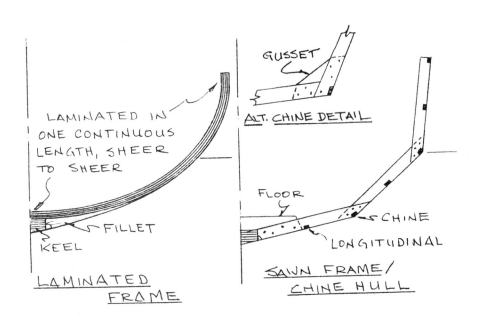

which case these pieces are joined by cleats at the butt ends. With double-sawn frames the parts overlap and are glued and fastened together so that cleats are not necessary. Preferable today are laminated frames formed of many layers of veneer glued together. If the frames are laminated doubly wide they can be sawn down the middle, making a perfect pair. Large boats may have one or more bent frames fitted between two sawn or laminated frames, while very large, heavy craft may use all sawn or laminated frames. An example of the latter is our recent 70-foot schooner *Tree of Life*, which has 2½-inch-by-4-inch laminated fir frames fitted every 14 inches.

Chine hulls use sawn frames almost exclusively, closely spaced for regular planking and more widely spaced if seam-batten planking is used. On a plywood hull longitudinal stringers are fitted. In powerboats with extreme flare in the forward sections it may be difficult to avoid cross-grain frames. In such instances, double-sawn frames or even laminated frames should be used.

Longitudinal framing that uses closely spaced longitudinal stringers on widely spaced sawn frames or bulkhead framing is excellent for laminated hulls as well as for plywood planking. In bulkhead framing, the major hull bulkheads and furniture are reinforced and supply the necessary transverse strength. Strip-planked hulls can also use bulkhead framing if the plank strips are increased in thickness, but if this is done it is rare to see longitudinal stringers.

Composite construction, popular in high-quality wood yachts in the 1930s, is rarely seen today. In this form of construction, the wood planking, usually regular caulked planking, is bolted to steel or bronze angle frames. Steel frames were usually galvanized, but the very highest quality craft used bronze for its durability. Composite construction is very strong but relatively costly. With modern glues, laminated frames make more sense for today's yachts.

Fastenings

Electrolysis can be a dangerous problem in boats. Wooden boats, with their many and different kinds of fastenings, are at risk. Galvanized iron or other ferrous metals must not be mixed with bronze fastenings or lead keels. Lead-ballast keels should be fastened with bronze or monel bolts, never with galvanized iron or stainless steel bolts. Stainless steel is less noble than lead and subject to crevice corrosion if fitted below water, and therefore not the ideal material for keel bolts, rudder stocks, or propeller shafts. Bronze and monel are more costly, so stainless steel keel bolts are common on modern yachts, but they have caused the loss of more than one keel. Bronze fastenings should never be used with aluminum hardware or masts because the two metals form a battery that corrodes the aluminum. Stainless fastenings, well bedded, are the only choice in that case, but even they need to be inspected regularly.

Even if all fastenings and fittings are of identical metal, problems can occur due to stray electrical currents that may cause deterioration of the hull metals. Sacrificial zinc plates should be fitted to the hull at all major metal points (shafts, through-hulls, rudder fittings, etc.) so the zinc is eaten away instead of the costly fittings. Many designers and builders recommend a complete bonding system. In this installation all major metal parts and, in particular, all through-hull metals are connected by #8 AWG copper wire to a central copper bonding strip that, in turn, is connected to the ballast keel or to a grounding plate on the outside of the hull. Such a bonding system provides lightning protection as well as a degree of electrolysis protection.

Decks

The tightest deck for a wooden hull is marine plywood. It is also the lightest, strongest, and easiest to maintain. Laid teak decks, as seen on high-quality yachts, provide excellent footing along with beautiful appearance, but have many drawbacks. They develop leaks, require much more care, often require refastening, and are not as tight as plywood. It is common to see a teak deck laid over a plywood subdeck, providing the appearance of teak with the strength and tightness of plywood. However, a leak in the teak overlayer may be hard to trace because water can run between the layers, if they are not perfectly bedded, and drip into the cabin many feet from where it enters the teak-planked deck. Such construction is very prone to rot because the water lies between the layers, keeping the plywood continually damp. Eventually, massive repair work is necessary.

Strip-planked decks are also quite feasible and are tight and strong. They can be oil finished for good footing and good appearance and, generally, treated as the laid fir or pine decks you see on some large craft. Older construction methods may use tongue-and-groove decking covered with canvas laid in glue or white lead, but this method is inferior to plywood or strip-planked decks.

Plywood Hulls

The same features that make plywood an excellent decking material also make it an excellent hull material, but *only* if the hull is of suitable shape. Any sheet material bends only in one direction, so plywood is unsuitable for round-bilge carvel hulls unless it is ripped up into planks, which defeats the purpose. What is not realized by most amateur builders is that plywood is also unsuitable for chine hulls that have a great deal of twist in the sections. Where there is great twist, the hull must be designed by multiconic development if the plywood planking is going to fit properly to the forward frames. If you are not certain that a design can be plywood planked, check with

the architect before purchasing the plans.

I have designed several multiconic plywood hulls where the bottom sections were so rounded forward that the chine faired almost invisibly into the topsides. These boats have triple-planked bottoms of three layers of ¼-inch plywood, so the builder does not have to force a hard bend into heavy plywood.

The butts are a weak point in a plywood hull because the bottom or topsides have a seam all the way across. Usually a wide plywood doubler is fitted inside the joint, and, while strong, it can create hard spots in the hull if not carefully done. A well-made scarf joint is much better in this respect, or, on larger hulls, several layers of plywood can be used with the butts well staggered.

Another problem with plywood is that, when painted, it looks like plywood. Careful sealing and priming are necessary to prevent lifting of the grain. An epoxy sealer helps to reduce this problem. Plywood is available with resin surfaces, and this material can give an excellent paint job on interior surfaces. However, I prefer a Formica finish for real durability and zero maintenance.

Home craftsmen often wonder whether they should use exterior- or marine-grade plywood. Both grades are glued with the same waterproof resin glue, but exterior-grade plywood has voids (holes) in the inner surfaces, while marine-grade has the voids filled. Marine-grade plywood should be used for all exterior surfaces. It should also be used where the edge shows, because otherwise a void might mar the finish. Exterior-grade plywood is suitable for interior joinerwork and the sublayer of cabin soles that are to have a teak plywood overlay, and is commonly used for these purposes by many production builders. Many plywood boats have been built of exterior-grade plywood throughout and have given good service for a number of years, but if you are going to put all that labor into building your own boat, it makes good sense to use the higher-grade material for the hull.

Metal Boats

Metal hulls, both aluminum and steel, are becoming more popular every year due to their strength, durability, low cost (steel), and light weight (aluminum). Chine hulls have always been fairly common in metal, but round-bilge hulls were rarely seen in North America (although they have been popular in Europe since the 1920s) because they require skills and equipment possessed by only a few of the better boatyards.

This changed in the mid 1970s when Brewer Yacht Designs pioneered the radius-bilge hull. This is essentially a single-chine hull that uses very large radius sections between the flat topsides and bottom. This radius can taper gradually from 2 feet aft to 4 feet or more forward. The resulting yachts are difficult to tell from a pure round-bilge vessel. Other designers have used a radius bilge, but some use the same radius from bow to stern, and this does not produce as handsome a hull in my opinion. Radius-bilge hulls are not all that difficult to build and are quite suitable to a small metal-fabricating yard. Even amateurs have completed 45-footers and larger craft of our design in both steel and aluminum.

Basic Construction

Metal hulls are framed with either bent frames of angular or T-shape sections, or sawn, flat-bar frames set athwartship. Older craft used all athwartship frames, closely spaced. Modern construction favors widely spaced transverse frames with closely spaced longitudinal stringers to support the plating. Indeed,

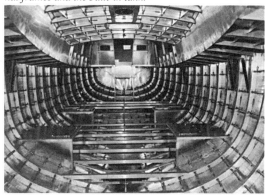

The aluminum sailing yacht Troubador *shows off her interior framing, looking aft. Notice the closely spaced longitudinal frames and the built-in tank.*

on our latest designs the longitudinals are set proud of the transverse frames, and the plating is not welded to the latter at all. This produces a very fair hull, with none of the starved-dog look of the athwartship-framed vessel, because the longitudinal stringers eliminate the tendency of the plating to sag between the frames.

Fastening today in both steel and aluminum is done almost completely by welding. The exceptions are thinly plated aluminum outboard boats, which are often riveted. The advantage of the all-welded hull is that it is a one-piece, seamless structure with great strength and complete watertight integrity.

Electrolysis is a problem in metal craft. Since both steel and aluminum react strongly with copper-based metals, bronze fittings must be avoided wherever possible. Stainless steel shafts and propellers are available with nonmetallic stern bearings, and fiberglass-reinforced nylon seacocks can substitute for bronze. A bronze fitting must be insulated from the hull metal with a Micarta block and fastened with stainless steel bolts. Similarly, bronze deck hardware should be replaced by aluminum or stainless where possible, but if it has to be used, it must be insulated from the hull with neoprene gaskets and fastened with stainless steel bolts.

Decks

Metal decks make the most sense on metal hulls, although the traditionalist might consider a heavy teak deck bolted to angle beams. I do not like teak decks laid over solid metal decks for the same reason that I do not like teak laid over plywood subdecks. The teak overlay deck makes even less sense with a metal subdeck since it requires drilling thousands of holes through what was a watertight metal deck. This is asking for trouble somewhere down the canal.

The best deck finish for a metal hull is a nonskid rubber or plastic material, available in attractive colors, simply glued in place. Another good choice is a painted deck with nonskid material mixed into the final coat. If you must have a teak overlay deck there are methods of accomplishing it, none of them inexpensive or perfect, but they are beyond the scope of this volume. Consult a first-class builder.

It is not uncommon to see aluminum cabins, or even decks, on steel hulls. The advantages are the weight saved, the boat's lower center of gravity, and the reduced maintenance in heavy wear areas. The construction can be accomplished by a bolted joint with a neoprene gasket and closely spaced stainless bolts. An alternate is a metal bar, composed of steel bonded to aluminum under explosive pressure, that permits a welded joint to be made. Both methods are costly in labor and material and are not feasible for the average craft.

Steel

Steel is an excellent material for construction where low cost is paramount. It is, indeed, the least costly of all materials for a one-off yacht or workboat—about 20% less than wood construction and as much as 40% less than aluminum. Another big advantage of steel is its strength. It is the strongest of all the common boatbuilding materials, and has a tensile strength of about 55,000 pounds per square inch. Steel also has the ability to stretch 30 to 40% before it fails; collisions and groundings that would destroy a wood or fiberglass hull often result only in deep dents in a steel boat. Steel does not deteriorate with age, if it is protected from the elements, and it is fireproof—although that is small compensation if the wood furniture is all burned out.

The problem with steel is that it makes a heavy boat. Steel shows a big disadvantage in weight for conventional craft under 45 to 50 feet because it is not possible to employ plating thinner than ⅛ inch and still produce a fair hull. Consider that ⅛ inch steel plate, about what would be used on a 30-footer, weighs as much as 1⅝ inch mahogany, ⅜ inch aluminum, or ⁹⁄₁₆ inch fiberglass, and the problem becomes evident.

Steel also rusts if it is not protected from the elements. Modern coating systems go a long way toward solving this problem. I have seen steel yachts that have sailed thousands of miles and still look new. The labor involved in the careful preparation of the surface, both inside and out, is costly, and the very expensive materials add to the cost. Despite this, steel craft are still the least costly to build in the first place, and the maintenance over the years is really no more than that of a good wooden yacht.

Aluminum

Aluminum is one of the finest materials for boatbuilding, but its cost is about 20% or more higher than that of a comparable wooden craft. The advantages of aluminum are lightness, corrosion resistance, and strength. When this is balanced against the added cost, aluminum can be an attractive material, particularly when the higher resale values of aluminum boats are considered.

The fully developed aluminum hull of Troubador, *on her way to have the interior fitted.*

Aluminum is only one-third the weight of steel, so a plating thickness double that of steel can be used on an aluminum boat with a weight savings of about 50%. Aluminum is not as strong as steel, having a tensile strength of about 35,000 psi, but it is certainly adequate for all normal boatbuilding purposes. And of course, the aluminum boat can have thicker plating to make it virtually as strong as steel, yet still save considerable weight. Some years ago I designed a 55-foot aluminum motorsailer to replace a 50-foot steel vessel. The larger aluminum craft weighed only 60,000 pounds, compared to 90,000 pounds for the steel yacht. The improvement in performance was substantial.

The modern 5000 series alloys must be used for all exterior parts of the vessel, particularly those in constant contact with seawater, because these materials are basically inert in seawater. Indeed, they do not have to be painted, and many aluminum boats are sailing the waters as naked as the day they were launched. Of course, they still need antifouling bottom paint to keep pesky barnacles and grass under control. Other alloys, such as 6061-T6, are used for extruded items such as aluminum masts, and often for interior framing angles and longitudinals because of their greater stiffness. However, they must be protected from seawater by paint or anodizing and must never be used for hull plating or other exterior parts.

If it is to be painted, the aluminum vessel also needs very careful and costly preparation and modern epoxy or synthetic finishes. On the other hand, the interior of the hull can be left bare since there will be no deterioration of the metal.

Insulation

If metal hulls are not thoroughly insulated they will be cold and noisy and have condensation problems. The most common insulation is sprayed-in-place foam, but it can burn, and the fumes are poisonous. On the other hand, it does seal off moisture from the hull and can be beneficial to a steel vessel as it does much to prevent rusting from the inside. It is commonly used in steel craft as a result.

Aluminum boats can use a glued-in-place neoprene foam that is much less flammable than sprayed foam and easier to remove if repairs are necessary. I have used the pink, foil-backed fiberglass insulation in some cases, and it has worked well. It is nonflammable, easy to install, easily removed when necessary, and inexpensive. That's hard to beat.

Fiberglass-Reinforced Plastic (FRP)

The majority of stock production boats built today are of FRP construction (fiberglass for short), using polyester resin as a binder. Fiberglass boats are long lived, tough, relatively inexpensive, and require minimum maintenance. The usual production hull is a hand layup of solid fiberglass and resin and may be from ³⁄₁₆ inch to 1 inch or more in thickness.

Fiberglass Materials

The fiberglass used in boatbuilding is made up of several basic types, including cloth, woven roving, and mat. Each type is available in different thicknesses. *Cloth* is a finely woven material and is both thin and strong. It is used where high strength is

The hull of a fiberglass Jason, fresh from the mold.

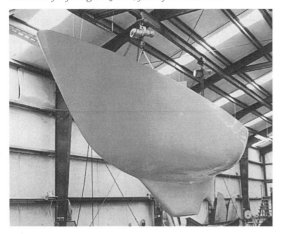

Chopped-strand mat (2 ¼-ounce). (From The Fiberglass Boat Repair Manual, *by Allan Vaitses. International Marine, 1988)*

Woven roving (18-ounce). (From The Fiberglass Boat Repair Manual, *by Allan Vaitses. International Marine, 1988)*

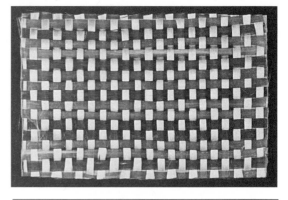

Lightweight woven roving (8.2-ounce). (From The Fiberglass Boat Repair Manual, *by Allan Vaitses. International Marine, 1988)*

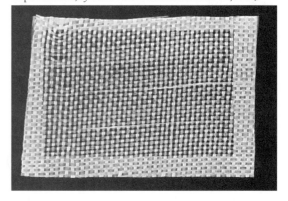

required and, sometimes, to give a smooth outer finish. *Woven roving* is a much coarser weave, thicker than cloth but also very strong. It is used in the average boat to build up strength quickly. *Mat* is formed of chopped glass and has relatively little tensile strength. Low-quality FRP boats may be made of an all-mat laminate, often with the resin sprayed from chopper guns rather than laid up by hand. Better-quality craft are usually laminated from alternating layers of mat and woven roving. The mat gives thickness and stiffness to the laminate and bonds the layers of woven roving together.

This is a very simplified explanation, and there are other forms of fiberglass reinforcing, such as Fabmat (a combination of mat and woven roving) and high-strength reinforcing materials such as unidirectional fibers, E-glass, and S-glass. The average FRP boat, however, is built of mat and woven roving, and this is particularly true of the thousands of craft that have been imported from the Far East. Ocean racers, both power and sail, often incorporate some extremely costly and high-strength materials, such as kevlar or carbon fiber, into the laminate at high-stress areas.

FRP hulls are weak in flexural strength and need to be stiffened by adequate framing. In production

These eight squares of mat and woven roving represent a typical fiberglass laminate with a finished thickness of approximately ⁵⁄₁₆ inch. Laid up in a mold, the laminate schedule reads, in order of application (left to right): gelcoat (not pictured) mat, mat, roving, mat, roving, mat, roving, mat. (From The Fiberglass Boat Repair Manual, *by Allan Vaitses. International Marine, 1988)*

This laminate uses alternating mat and unidirectional roving; the two layers of the latter are laid at 90 degrees to each other. The schedule (left to right) is gelcoat (not pictured), mat, mat, roving, roving, mat; its thickness would finish ³⁄₁₆ to ¼ inch. (From The Fiberglass Boat Repair Manual, *by Allan Vaitses. International Marine, 1988)*

Bonded mat and roving. In the Fabmat 1-ounce mat is backed with 10-ounce woven roving, the pattern of which can be seen faintly. (From The Fiberglass Boat Repair Manual, *by Allan Vaitses. International Marine, 1988)*

Unidirectional roving (13-ounce). (From The Fiberglass Boat Repair Manual, *by Allan Vaitses. International Marine, 1988)*

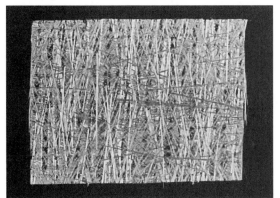

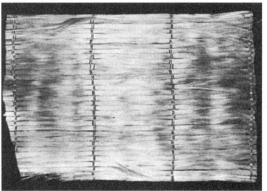

CONSTRUCTION

FIGURE 10-3

Use of a fillet of foam between the bulkhead and the hull prevents a ridge from printing through the hull, and eases the curve for taping. (From The Fiberglass Boat Repair Manual, *by Allan Vaitses. International Marine, 1988)*

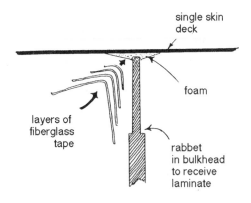

FIGURE 10-4

Solid fiberglass hull liner, showing limited accessibility of the hull for repair. Sometimes the liners is made up of subassemblies, particularly in the head area; these can ease access. The headliner is almost always a separate molding. (From The Fiberglass Boat Repair Manual, *by Allan Vaitses. International Marine, 1988)*

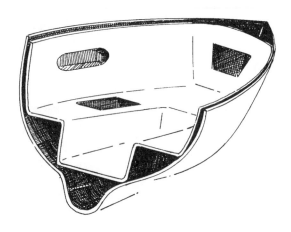

FRP boats this is generally accomplished by plywood bulkheads and joinerwork, which are bonded in place by fiberglass tape. Some builders use a complete FRP interior pan that forms the cabin sole and much of the furniture, and which is then taped into place to reinforce the basic hull. A distinct disadvantage of this interior pan is that it may make it difficult to inspect or repair the interior of the hull.

Resin and Blisters

The most common resin in use is polyester resin. However, polyester resin can result in blisters forming below the waterline in the gelcoat after a few years of use. Today many builders use an outer layer of vinylester resin to reduce the chance of blistering, and then finish up the rest of the laminate with the less costly polyester.

Epoxy resin is superior to polyester resin. It is more watertight and more durable, but it is expensive and severely irritating to the skin of the workers.

For these reasons it is not used on production boats. It is increasingly used as a final coat over polyester-bonded FRP craft to reduce or eliminate blistering. Also, epoxy is the resin of choice for bonding fiberglass cloth to a wood hull, as well as for gluing and coating laminated wood vessels.

Cores

Cored FRP panels are stronger than single-skin FRP panels of equal weight. The core, laid in between the inner and outer laminates of glass, acts like the web in an I-beam and contributes to stiffness as well as adding both sound and temperature insulation. Coring is used in large, flat areas such as decks and cabin roofs, and is also used to build many light, strong hulls.

Many different materials have been used for cores. One of the most common is edge-grain balsa wood.

FIGURE 10-5
Variations of fiberglass hull/deck joints.

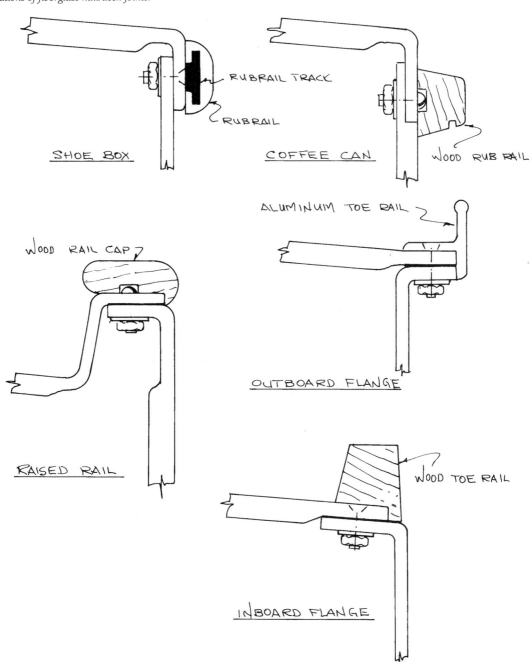

SHOE BOX

RUBRAIL TRACK

RUBRAIL

COFFEE CAN

WOOD RUB RAIL

ALUMINUM TOE RAIL

WOOD RAIL CAP

OUTBOARD FLANGE

RAISED RAIL

WOOD TOE RAIL

INBOARD FLANGE

FIGURE 10-6

Typical cored hull layup.

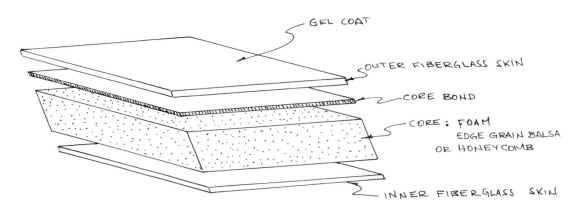

This is most often used as a stiffener in deck laminates, but it is also used in hulls, usually racing hulls, where stiffness and light weight are prime considerations. There has been concern that the balsa core can rot if water gets to it through a crack in the outer laminate. However, the small squares of wood are separated from each other by resin if the work is done properly, so that rot cannot spread easily.

Expanded PVC foam cores such as Airex, Termanto, and Klegecell have proven themselves as well. They are inert materials and cannot absorb water and rot if the outer skin is broken. They also are available in large panels that lend themselves to one-off construction over a relatively simple wood framework.

Core materials vary in thickness according to boat size and may range from 1/4 inch to 1 inch. Very large hulls may have two layers of coring with a thin layer of fiberglass between to bond the cores together.

A few boats have been built with a wood core, usually a strip-planked hull with no framing and fairly thin planking. The FRP covering, both inside and out, protects the wood core and provides sufficient additional strength to render the hull a solid, one-piece unit. Bulkheads are fitted and fastened to the hull with FRP tape, similar to the system used in production craft. This construction lends itself to the amateur builder because the large timbers of wood boats and the intricate molds of fiberglass hulls are eliminated.

FIGURE 10-7

Not all areas of a hull or deck are cored. (From The Fiberglass Boat Repair Manual, *by Allan Vaitses. International Marine, 1988)*

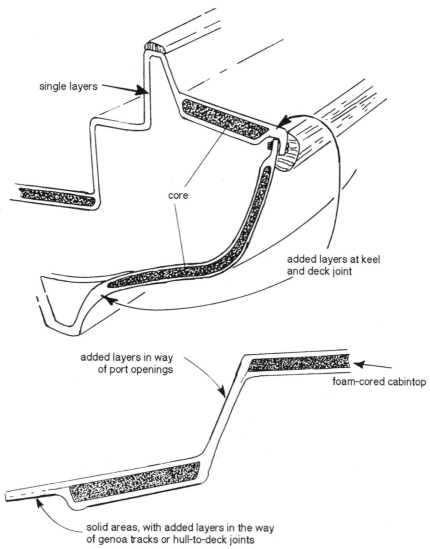

single layers

core

added layers at keel
and deck joint

added layers in way
of port openings

foam-cored cabintop

solid areas, with added layers in the way
of genoa tracks or hull-to-deck joints

CHAPTER ELEVEN

Plans, The Designer, and You

The Plans Packet

Boat plans are drawn to scales ranging from $\frac{1}{10}$ to $\frac{1}{32}$ full size; generally, the larger the boat, the smaller the scale. The following drawings constitute a complete set of plans for the average yacht.

Lines Drawing

We have discussed the lines to some extent, and the interpretation of the shapes. The lines drawing consists of the profile view showing the sheerline, buttocks, chine, and keel. The lines drawing also includes the plan view showing the waterlines (and, in some cases, the diagonals) and the body sections. The sections may be superimposed over the profile view or drawn off to one side. Computer-derived lines drawings may have a three-dimensional view of the hull off to one side also. This view is not very useful to anyone, but it looks pretty and impresses clients. I do it whenever I can.

The drawing may include the offset table, although this may be on a separate piece of paper. Offsets are the dimensions from the centerline, the load waterline, or a baseline to the intersections of the waterlines, buttocks, and diagonals at each station. In the United States, the offsets are expressed in feet, inches, and eighths of inches; thus 6 feet 3½ inches is expressed as 6.3.4. A + sign is used to indicate an extra $\frac{1}{16}$ inch, so 6.3.4+ would be read as 6 feet 3⁹⁄₁₆ inches. The rest of the world expresses the offsets in the metric system, of course.

Construction Drawings

The complete construction drawings consist of the inboard-construction profile, the deck-framing plan, one or more sections through the yacht showing the construction at different places, and on some hulls, a bottom-framing plan. These drawings show the sizes of all the major parts, the size and location of major fastenings, molded parts in the case of a FRP vessel, and the bigger items of machinery, including engines, tanks, generators, water heaters, etc. The construction drawing often includes large-scale detail sketches of rudder bearings, special joinerwork, tanks, and other items of special importance. Sometimes detail sketches are on separate sheets. Large craft may have an engine-room drawing showing the location of all the auxiliary machinery, batteries, shafting, and other gear. Sailboat construction drawings have separate drawings of the chainplates, stemhead fittings, centerboard and case, and other specific items.

Accommodation Plans

The drawings of the interior arrangement consist of the layout plan (a bird's-eye view of the interior with the deck removed), the inboard profile (usually the port side), and as many cross sections as necessary to show the details of the joinerwork throughout the boat. On vessels with complex interiors, both port and starboard interior profiles are shown (Figure 11-1).

Sail Plan or Outboard Profile

Powerboats have an outboard-profile drawing that shows the appearance of the completed yacht. Sailing craft show this on the sail plan, which also details the location, sizes, and other specifics of the spars, rigging, and sails.

Spar Drawing

Sailboats require spar drawings showing spreader lengths, heights, angles, winch and cleat locations, and other important information. For large craft, spar drawings are often separate; for smaller boats they are usually placed on the sail plan. If the spars are wood, or in case of a gaff rig, there should be separate drawings detailing the spar dimensions, constructions, tangs, and fittings.

Deck Plan

The deck plan may be omitted for small powerboats if sufficient detail is given on the outboard profile and accommodation plan, but sailboats should have a deck drawing showing the size, type, and location of winches, cleats, sail tracks, and other hardware.

Miscellaneous

Other drawings may be supplied as required. Sailing craft may have large-scale lines drawings of a fin keel or ballast casting, complete with an offset table. Other drawings supplied depend upon the size and complexity of the vessel, and upon the cost of the plans. These can include plumbing and electrical drawings, as well as other major details.

Specifications

Most designs are accompanied by a set of written specifications containing general details of construction and equipment and other data not shown on the plans. There should also be a list of glue, fastenings, timber sizes, engine specifications, plumbing and wiring details, paint schedule, equipment, and other details. Unusual construction or design features may be explained in detail as well.

Custom or Stock Plans?

A stock plan is a plan the designer has available to anyone who may request it. It is often a vessel that was designed as a custom boat for another client, or it may be a plan the designer created in response to a general demand for a particular size and style of boat. The cost of stock designs vary widely from designer to designer; one designer may ask $100 for a stock 30-footer while another demands $3000 for a similar boat. The price often depends on the amount of detail, but too often it depends on the designer's reputation and ego.

FIGURE 11-1

The joiner sections show how the arrangement fits into various sections of the hull.

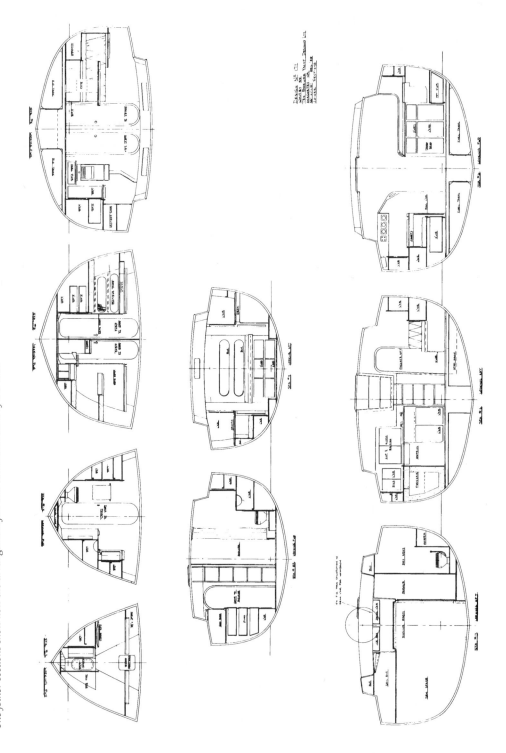

UNDERSTANDING BOAT DESIGN

Custom plans, as the name implies, are plans designed to suit the specific requirements of a client. The cost of custom plans is much more than for stock plans, but they are still very reasonably priced considering the total cost of a custom yacht. My office tries to keep the fee at about 4 or 5% of the cost of the completed vessel, although this is not always possible on unusual designs, or on craft that involve complex and detailed drawings.

With a custom design, the naval architect can afford to give the owner and builder consultation, advice, special sketches, and other assistance whenever required. This is rarely possible with stock plans, although most architects will bend over backward to help a dedicated amateur craftsman. With a custom design, the architect may also attend sea trials or even oversee the construction of the vessel if the owner desires. Another advantage of a custom design is that the designer, by making use of modern construction methods and materials, may save the owner substantial money in the long run, since stock plans are often dated, or do not include cost-saving details, or both.

The choice between buying a stock plan or a custom plan is easily made. If you find a stock plan from a reputable designer that meets your needs as to size, type, accommodations, construction, and performance without requiring major changes, then use it. Otherwise, a custom design is a better investment.

Selecting a Designer

It is important to select a reputable designer, but it is equally important that he or she is knowledgeable in the type of vessel you intend to build. Many designers have experience in power and sail, yachts and commercial craft, metal, wood, and fiberglass construction. However, some architects specialize in specific types of boats: ocean-racing sail, power, multihulls, hydroplanes, fishing craft—wherever their chief interest lies. In short, you cannot pick a yacht designer out of the yellow pages. It takes a bit of research. It is helpful to leaf through the yachting periodicals. The design sections of yachting magazines used to show examples of the latest craft from the boards of several architects, but in these tight economic times they are included less often, as the magazines concentrate on mass-produced boats instead. This is unfortunate. Two magazines that do cater to custom designs or amateur builders are *Sailing* and *Boatbuilder*. Their design sections still include material of interest to the serious yachtsman and are not simply a free plug for their advertisers. Even if you find nothing in the design sections of the magazines that meets your needs, you may find a designer whose style appeals to you.

The prospective owner who writes in detail about the size, type, rig, layout, performance, and other features of his dream ship, and advises the designer of his preferences as to construction, probable usage, and any other information along these lines, helps the designer serve him better. Such a letter receives a more considered reply than one asking simply for "plans of a 30-foot boat."

If you go ahead with a custom design, the designer should tell you exactly what drawings are included for the quoted fee or the hourly rate. He should also explain other services—such as inspections, trial trips, and equipment purchasing—that are included. A retainer to cover the cost of the preliminary sketches is customary. It is usually applied to the design fee once the preliminaries are accepted.

Preliminaries are small-scale drawings of the outboard profile, accommodations, and, perhaps, a sketchy lines drawing illustrating the designer's interpretation of the client's needs. This is the stage of the design where suggestions and changes are welcomed by the designer, *not* when the design is half completed. Once the owner accepts the final preliminaries, the designer should be able to proceed with the drawings, confident that there will be no major changes in the client's requirements. If such changes do occur, the designer has every right to charge for the work. Once we were ready to ask for bids on a new center-cockpit cutter when the client decided he wanted a pilothouse boat instead. Virtually every drawing except the lines had to be completely redone; fortunately, the client understood the problem and agreed to the extra charges.

Stock plans are available immediately when the design fee is paid, but custom plans may take from two to twelve months or longer, depending upon the size of the vessel. Often a stock design may meet most of your requirements, but need some alterations to satisfy your specific needs. Too many good designs have been ruined because the owner wanted more headroom or a longer cabin, and decided to do the work himself. It is essential to consult with the designer if you contemplate any changes, except minor alterations to cabin or deck arrangements that *involve no changes to major weights.*

A risk in stock plans is that the design may be old and include outdated construction methods that run up the cost. One stock design for a famous double-ended ketch requires such heavy timbers that you would have to own an oak forest to afford to build it at today's prices. A modern, laminated version could be built for 75% of the original design's cost, and it would be easier to maintain, live longer, and perform better.

If you are a good draftsman and can work up the changes yourself, you may save some money, but have the final changes approved by the architect before you incorporate them into your boat. Remember, alterations cost money. If you can't find a stock design that suits you it may be wiser to invest in a custom design right from the start.

Modifying Your Boat

If you are already a boat owner, you may be interested in alterations that would improve the comfort or performance of your vessel. There are often many beneficial changes that can be made. Boats down by the stern or bow can be trimmed by shifting ballast or relocating heavy weights such as tanks or batteries. Power craft with snappy rolls can have weights shifted outboard from the centerline to slow the motion. Powerboats with a tendency to squat by the stern at speed can be improved by the addition of trim tabs or wedges. Recently we modified the shape of a popular fiberglass 45-foot powerboat, changing it from a round-bilge to a chine hull by the use of structural foam and fiberglass, increasing speed by 10% and greatly reducing the size of the stern wave.

Sailing yachts can gain stability by relocating weight from the spars, rigs, and upperworks to the bilges. Rudder shapes are often open to improvement, as are fin keels. Many older yachts can gain by improvements to rigging, or by replacing their wood spars with aluminum to save weight aloft.

There are many areas for experimentation, and trying out new ideas can be one of the greatest joys of boating. However, if major changes are contemplated an architect should be consulted. This is particularly true if the changes involve a permanent feature such as tanks or spars. A yacht designer can calculate the effect on trim of shifting heavy weights and, where necessary, compensate for it. The architect is also in a position to give advice on rig changes that may improve a boat's performance or reduce its handicap rating. Powerboat owners can benefit from a designer's advice on propeller selection and repowering. Unless you have training as an engineer, it is wise to consult with an architect on any permanent changes that could involve the trim, stability, or performance of the yacht.

Learning Small-craft Design

The yachtsman who is interested in learning about small-craft design has three possible roads to travel. The hobbyist can simply read about yacht design. Although this approach may seem simple, it is often difficult and confusing. There are very good books on the subject by Frances Kinney, Howard Chapelle, and others, but the difficulty lies in separating the wheat from the chaff. Practical experience is essential as the authors, including me, may push their own conception of the perfect hull, layout, or rig. It is important to develop your own ideas based on facts and experience, rather than to simply accept someone else's theories. For a start, see the recommended reading list at the back of this book.

The second road is open to both hobbyist and serious student. It is the home-study course. The cost is moderate, but large enough to keep the student working hard at it. Home-study courses start with the basics and work up to complete designs with an emphasis on standard small-craft design and construction. The Westlawn course is good, if it is done properly without taking all the easiest options. The Westlawn course requires a serious commitment in time and effort, but provides a thorough grounding in small-boat design.

The third method is for the serious student only. It is the time-honored college degree from the Webb Institute, M.I.T., Michigan, or another university offering a degree in naval architecture. Since the emphasis of the university course is on large-ship design, it is not ideal for students of small-boat design, but it does work. Many famous yacht designers have gone that route. The Maine Maritime Academy offers a course in small-craft design that is worth serious consideration as well.

Anyone going into the yacht design business should work as a draftsman or assistant for a reputable naval architect for several years to gain practical experience. This is true for university and home-study graduates. Indeed, it is best if the budding designer works for several different architects or builders before he hangs out his shingle, because he will gain invaluable experience and practical knowledge from each.

CHAPTER TWELVE

Amateur Boatbuilding

All that has gone before in this book contributes to the overall understanding of boatbuilding. It has given you a basic knowledge of hull types, characteristics, materials, and construction. Nothing, though, can substitute for going out on different boats, looking at them in boatyards, reading and studying plans and books, and talking to boat owners. If you need more information on any element of boating and boatbuilding, there are excellent books on the subject that are listed at the end of this section. What I can do here, for the amateur boatbuilder, is to say a few words about the state of the art that may guide you toward a successful and rewarding project.

People build their own boat for various reasons, but saving money is probably foremost. The labor cost in custom boatbuilding is a large chunk of the overall cost. It can be one-third or more of the total. Also, if you build the boat in your own garage or shop, you save much of the cost of the professional builder's overhead. You also save the professional's profit, though in many boatshops this is a rather small and nebulous figure.

If you are not a skilled carpenter, you might consider taking a course before you tackle a boat. One of

our clients, a doctor, took a course in welding, and then went out and built a 45-foot steel cutter. That's a bit more than most of us would care to tackle, but many local colleges, adult education programs, and YMCAs offer courses in woodworking and are an excellent way for the ham-handed to gain experience. There are a number of excellent full-time courses in wooden-boat building, but by and large these courses are designed for people who want to make a career in the business.

Most amateur builders start with a small project, perhaps a dinghy (which they will need anyway), and then work up to their dream boat. Kits are available for a number of good dinghies and small sailing boats. They reduce the chances for serious error and are a fine introduction to boatbuilding.

Wood and fiberglass are the amateur builder's favorite materials, although steel is gaining rapidly in popularity. We have had a number of our aluminum designs successfully built by amateurs. Some of the finest wooden yachts I have ever seen have been built by skilled amateur craftsmen. They had the time and the desire to turn out perfection. If you would like to see what the competent amateur builder can do, then visit some of the wooden or antique boat shows that are held annually throughout the country. It could open your eyes.

A claimed advantage of fiberglass is that a semi-skilled workman can laminate a hull with a minimum of training and supervision. This may be true, but good carpentry skills are still required to finish up the interior joinerwork and the exterior wood trim. It would be terribly frustrating to turn out a good fiberglass hull and have it ruined by second-class joinerwork.

Time is the main thing the amateur gives to his boat in place of money, and the sensible allocation of that time is important. Hundreds of potentially good boats are abandoned every year because the builders tired of the labor as the projects dragged on beyond expectations. True, some amateur builders have stayed at it for ten years or more, but, in general, two or three years is a better goal. Beyond that the project can grow stale, and, in addition to your own disenchantment, there is always the possibility of divorce or your neighbors may run you out of town.

Dreams of building a boat for one-third of the cost of a similar commercial model are often shattered. The builder finds that he cannot buy materials and equipment at the same discounts as the professional, and generally ends up wasting more material than the professional. The trick is to shop carefully, hunt for bargains, and use your materials to their best advantage. In addition, space to build a boat can be expensive. You cannot build a 35-footer in the average garage. Glue and fiberglass resins require a heated space. Ample power for lights and tools is also necessary. In some areas, amateur builders have banded together to rent large buildings and to buy tools, materials, and equipment at discount prices.

One of the biggest fears of the amateur builder is lofting the boat. Lofting is simply redrawing the small-scale plans provided by the designer to full size by using the table of offsets supplied with the lines drawing. The patterns for the various parts of the vessel are made from this full-size drawing. Amateur builders often complain that they do not have the space or skills to loft the boat full size. My reply is always, "Well, in that case, you don't have the space or skills to build the boat either, so forget it!"

Some builders, afraid of lofting, purchase a set of patterns from designers who specialize in the amateur market. The problem here is that paper patterns stretch and shrink with changes in humidity; it is not impossible that the resulting boat may turn out to be unfair. Mylar patterns are more stable than paper patterns, but more costly. In any case, these pattern sets cover only the body sections and rarely show the hull full length. Without the full-length lofting it is still quite possible to produce unfair sheerlines. Nothing spoils the appearance of a boat faster. Lofting is not that difficult and is a superb way to learn a great deal more about the boat you are going to build. Give it a try.

Boat Plans for Amateurs

Too many plans intended for the amateur builder are for very simple, boxy boats touted for their simplicity of construction. That may be fine for those who possess only simplicity of mind or skills, but we have found that the average amateur builder is capable of much more. Provided the plans contain sufficient detail and the designer is willing to provide telephone consultation, and even special sketches if necessary to explain some part of the vessel, the amateur can produce professional results from professional plans.

There are thousands of stock plans available for boats, but many of these were designed 30 or more years ago. The problem with these older plans is that the material, machinery, and hardware are often dated. This is not too serious if the designer is still available for consultation. You should know, however, that some of the plans still sold to amateurs were drawn back in the days when boats were built like icebreakers; not only is this a waste of material (and money), but such boats tend to sail like slugs.

Since it takes as long to build a good design as it does a bad design, and the resale value of the good design is much higher, it behooves the amateur to be choosy in selecting a set of plans. The more you know about boats, the better you will be able to make the right choice. Consider this book a starter, and go on to read everything you can find about the kind of boat you want to build.

A Portfolio of
Brewer Designs

Design Number: 42
Name: **CAPE COD CATBOAT**

LOA	21'7"
LWL	20'0"
Beam	10'0"
Draft	2'3"
Displacement	5,850 lbs.
Sail Area	374 sq. ft.
Ballast	1,800 lbs. inside
Fuel	to suit
Water	to suit
Sail Area/Displ Ratio	18.4
Displ/Length Ratio	326.5

This chine version of the Cape Cod catboat (pages 106–107) has been the single most popular stock plan I have ever done. More than 300 have been built by professionals and amateurs, from Europe to Australia and points between. Construction is on the husky side with commercial 2 x 4 framing and heavy plywood planking for strength, durability and simplicity. There is nothing in this design that cannot be handled by a competent amateur builder.

Like all catboats, she provides very comfortable accommodations for her length. The cabin is quite spacious for a couple, and the huge cockpit can easily accommodate two under a boom tent for family cruising, or seat eight for a daysailing party.

Tremendous stability is inherent in the beamy catboat hull, and she has ample sail area to move her along in any weather. All halyards are led aft, and there are deep reefs for heavy going.

The boatman requiring an able, comfortable, and simple-to-build sailing cruiser would do well to give a catboat some serious consideration.

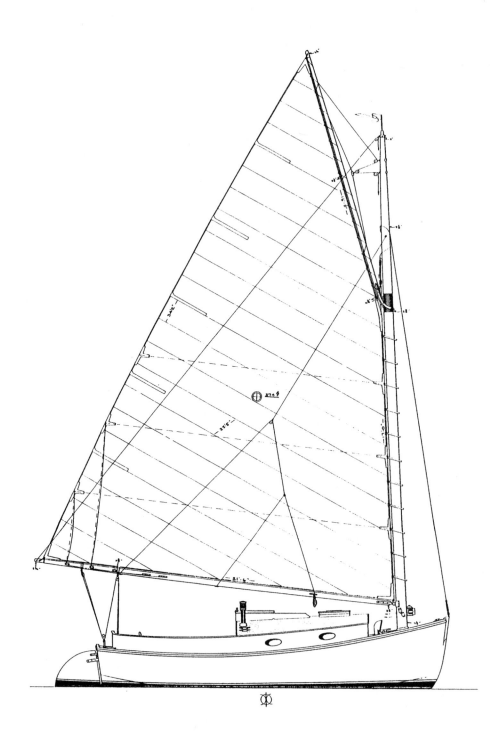

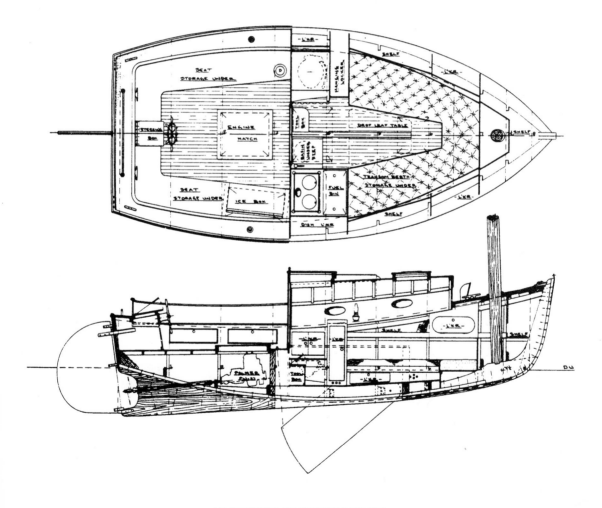

A PORTFOLIO OF BREWER DESIGNS

Design Number: 26
Name: **DEER ISLE 28**

LOA	28'2"
LWL	24'8"
Beam	9'6"
Draft	1'10"
Displacement	6,500 lbs.
Fuel	70 gals.
Water	20 gals.
Disp/Length Ratio	193

The plans of the Deer Isle 28 show workboat, sportfisherman, and cruiser versions and offer the amateur or professional wooden-boat builder a rugged, economical vessel that is simple to build and maintain, and with excellent seakeeping ability. She has been used for salmon fishing in Alaska, lobstering off New Hampshire, sport fishing in Mexico, and cruising everywhere.

Construction is of plywood planking on sawn longitudinal framing, bronze-fastened with Anchorfast nails. Because of the simplicity and ease of the planking, she is ideal for the home builder.

Power can be single or twin sterndrive engines, a conventional inboard installation, or single or twin outboards. One husky, commercially built 28 ran 800 miles from Washington to Alaska at an average of 20 knots powered by a single 200-h.p. outboard. This is a fast and able vessel in every way.

The accommodations provide a comfortable arrangement with a workable galley and an enclosed head. The cruiser version provides two additional berths in an after cabin. All in all, the Deer Isle 28 will provide her owner with a fast, comfortable, and inexpensive craft that will earn her keep over and over in utility and pleasure.

Plans for a 24-foot sistership are available.

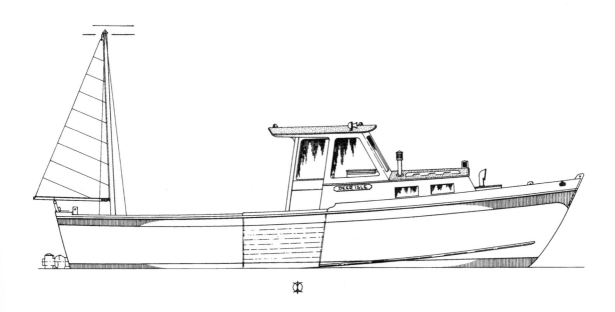

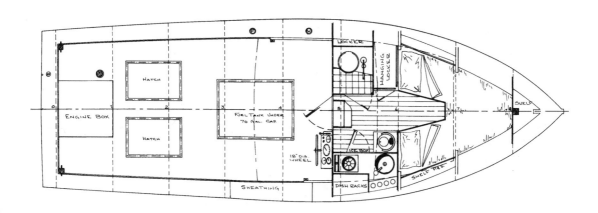

Design Number: 227
Name: **SWAGMAN**

LOA	33'9"
LWL	31'6"
Beam	11'1"
Draft	3'2"
Displacement	11,000 lbs.
Fuel	140 gals.
Water	to suit
Displ/Length Ratio	157

The Swagman name comes from the famous Australian song about the wandering hobo who "camped by the bilabong." This design gives much more than camping comfort with her three separate cabins, two heads, stall shower, and complete galley.

An unusual feature is the forward cockpit and walkaround foredeck, which will prove to be a popular spot in good weather. This deck is protected by high bulwarks and enables the helmsman to keep an eye on guests—and children. Indeed, a steering station can be fitted in the forward cockpit if desired so the skipper can be out there with them.

The steering station abaft the wheelhouse will be popular as well as it gives good visibility all around without the increased rolling motion of a high flying bridge.

Single or twin engines to 300-h.p. give flashing speeds and the first boat of this design has proved to be a fine performer in both smooth seas and rough water. The hull form features a high chine forward and a convex bottom shape for soft riding in a chop. A built-in spray rail and well-flared forward sections keep the spray down where it belongs.

Construction is of cored fiberglass to husky standards and is well suited to one-off methods. The design is well-suited to both competent amateur and professional builders with experience in fiberglass.

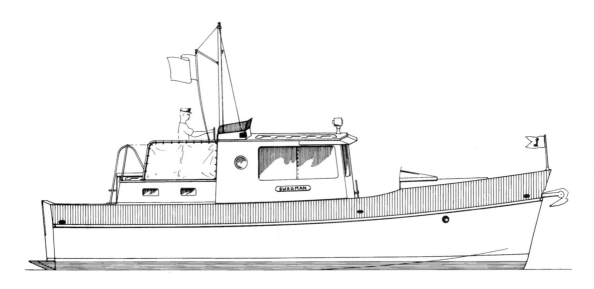

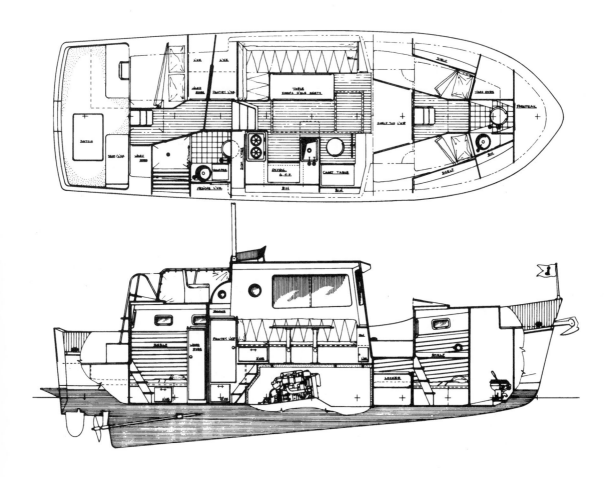

Design Number: 156
Name: ***MORGANE LE FAY***

LOA	33'10"
LWL	29'0"
Beam	11'0"
Draft	5'0'
Displacement	13,950 lbs.
Sail Area	618 sq. ft.
Ballast	5,350 lbs.
Fuel	25 gals.
Water	80 gals.
Sail Area/Displ Ratio	17.1
Displ/Length Ratio	255

This compact cruiser was designed for a client who required a seagoing vessel with excellent accommodations for a couple plus occasional guests.

The long waterline and generous sail area offer good all-around performance, while her fine entry and NACA fin assure excellent windward performance. Hull sections are firm with good deadrise for ease of motion in a seaway.

The interior provides a spacious galley and saloon area and *Morgane* gives a feeling of being larger than her 34 feet. There is generous stowage throughout, of course, as is essential on a yacht that will be used for extended voyaging.

The rig is well stayed with double spreaders, and runners are also fitted to tension the forestay on a long windward slog. Other seagoing aspects of the design include the husky windlass, double head rig, boom gallows, cockpit raft locker, deep dodger, and the protective windshield that gives a snug cockpit in dusty going.

Construction is of one-off fiberglass using any of the normal methods such as C-Flex or foam core. Ballast is outside and is strongly supported by deep floors.

In sum, *Morgane Le Fay* is a solid, good-performing cruiser that will be at home in coastal waters or on transocean voyages.

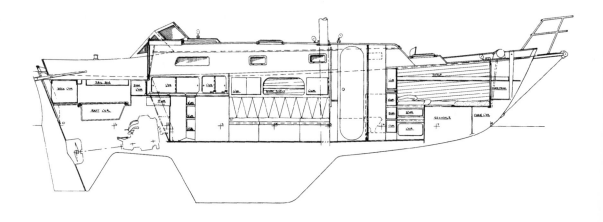

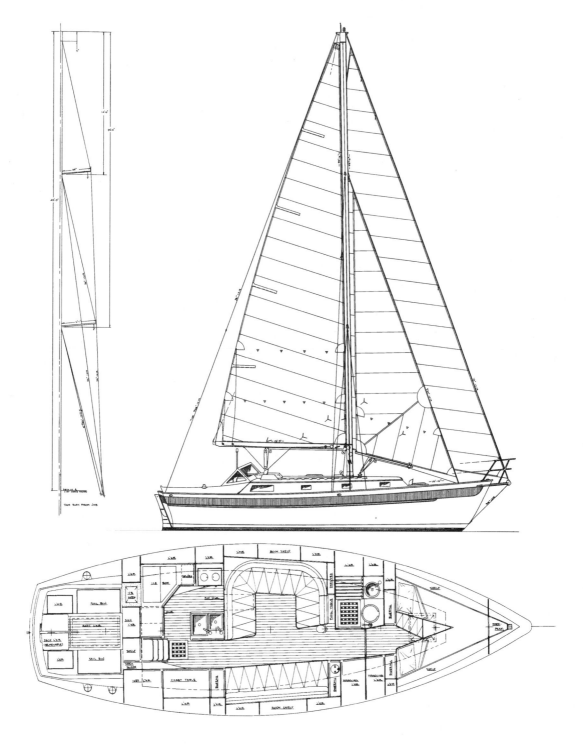

A PORTFOLIO OF BREWER DESIGNS

Design Number: 88
Name: *SUNSHINE*

LOA	34'5"
LWL	30'4"
Beam	11'4"
Draft	5'0"
Displacement	23,900 lbs.
Sail Area	742 sq. ft.
Ballast	10,000 lbs.
Fuel	100 gals.
Water	120 gals.
Sail Area/Displ Ratio	14.3
Displ/Length Ratio	382

Sunshine was designed for an East Coast yachtsman who was quite well known in the offshore racing circuit. She is not a racing yacht, obviously, but she is a very spacious and able cruiser that will attract a lot of attention in any port. The accommodations are comfortable for one or two couples, and the cockpit is large enough for big daysailing parties.

Sunshine features a full-keel, heavy-displacement hull, with a slow, easy motion in heavy seas and a steady helm. She is based on the Maine pinky sloops, sailing fishing boats noted for speed and seaworthiness.

The sail area may seem to be on the low side for her displacement, but the sail area/wetted surface ratio is still a good 2.0 so she will move along very nicely in light air. In moderate-heavy breezes *Sunshine* has the stability to carry full sail and really pick up her heels when other 35-footers are reefed down and making heavy going of it.

The fiberglass hull can be built by any of the usual one-off processes: C-Flex, foam core, etc., and it would be an easy project to convert her to strip planking on bulkhead framing, fiberglass covered. Her rig is straightforward, with solid wood spars and traditional rigging, and thus will not prove costly to set up.

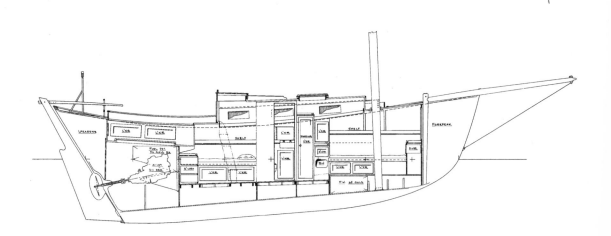

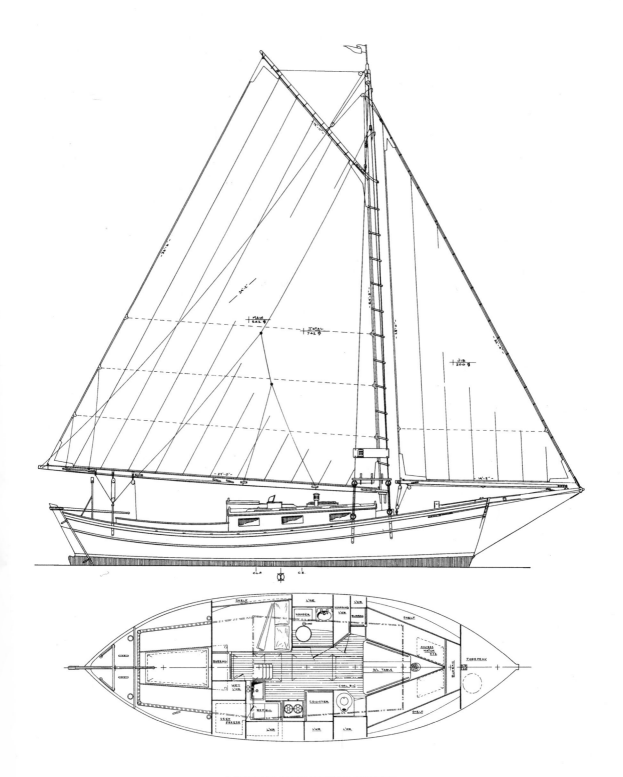

A PORTFOLIO OF BREWER DESIGNS

115

Design Number: 198
Name: **ARAGOSA 38**

LOA	38'1"
LWL	31'3"
Beam	12'5"
Draft	6'0"
Displacement	19,700 lbs.
Sail Area	756 sq. ft.
Ballast	6,900 lbs. lead
Fuel	45 gals.
Water	120 gals.
Sail Area/Displ Ratio	16.6
Displ/Length Ratio	288.2

The Aragosa 38 is a modern, radius-bilge steel yacht designed to perform well and to provide her crew with comfortable accommodations for extended cruising.

The fin-keel hull has a high-aspect-ratio, skeg-hung rudder for good directional stability and positive control. Construction is of closely spaced longitudinal stringers on transverse framing to ensure a strong and fair hull.

The tall rig spreads generous sail area for light wind conditions. Double spreaders and inboard chainplates allow close sheeting, so the 38 provides impressive windward performance.

The Aragosa's layout is not cramped with excessive berths but instead is designed to offer the amenities necessary for a very comfortable life aboard. Study the stall shower, bookcase, cabin heater, separate nav seat, U-shaped galley and generous stowage and you will see a yacht that is sensibly designed for long, safe, and comfortable voyages.

Many radius-bilge yachts of this general type have been successfully built by amateurs, and the 38 is well within the ability of the competent craftsman or the small shop. She provides her owner with a cruising yacht that combines comfort, performance, safety, and strength in a handsome package.

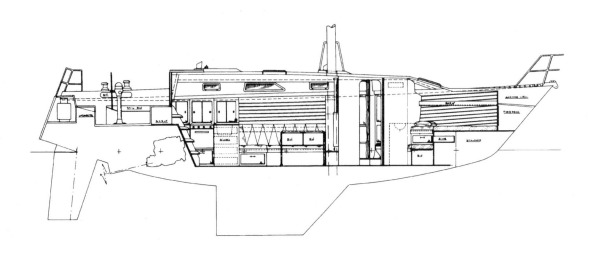

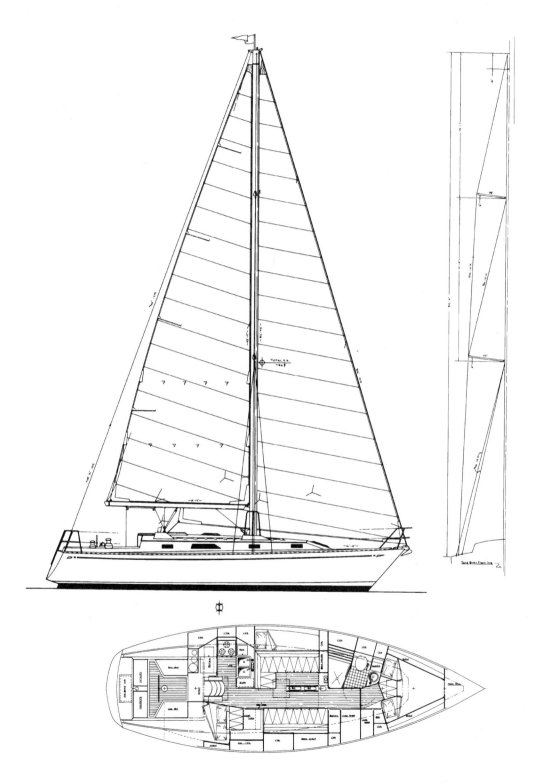

A PORTFOLIO OF BREWER DESIGNS

Design Number: 214
Name: *ORCA*

LOA	45'0"
LWL	38'0"
Beam	13'10"
Draft	5'11"
Displacement	39,000 lbs.
Sail Area	1,153 sq. ft.
Ballast	12,000 lbs.
Fuel	180 gals.
Water	160 gals.
Sail Area/Displ Ratio	16.04
Displ/Length Ratio	317

Orca was custom-designed for extensive, long-range cruising. Her construction calls for a steel hull with aluminum deck and superstructure; an all-steel version is certainly feasible, and all-aluminum would make a superb yacht.

She features our normal large radius-bilge hull combined with a moderately long fin and a skeg-hung rudder. The propeller is well protected from pot warps and logs by a small guard, while the shaft is strongly enclosed to ease the problem of lifting the boat with slings.

The arrangement provides two-cabin privacy for the owner and guests and features a large pilot-house/saloon with a nine-and-a-half-foot settee for comfortable lounging and entertaining. A spacious galley and a roomy head with separate stall shower assure convenience, while a washer/dryer fits under the berth in the forward cabin.

The tall cutter rig spreads good sail area, and *Orca* is a fine all-around performer. The mast is strongly supported by double spreaders, and running backstays can be set up in heavy weather to reduce mast panting. Lines are led aft for ease of handling.

A knowledgeable owner contributed many ideas to make *Orca* a first-class long-range cruiser, and she will prove to be a superbly comfortable coastal cruiser as well as an able bluewater voyager.

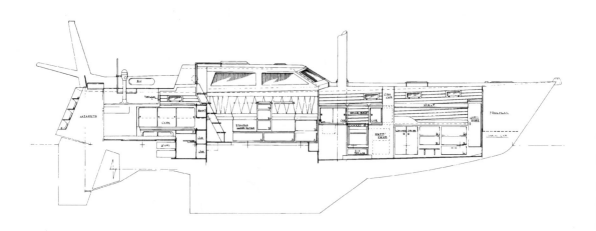

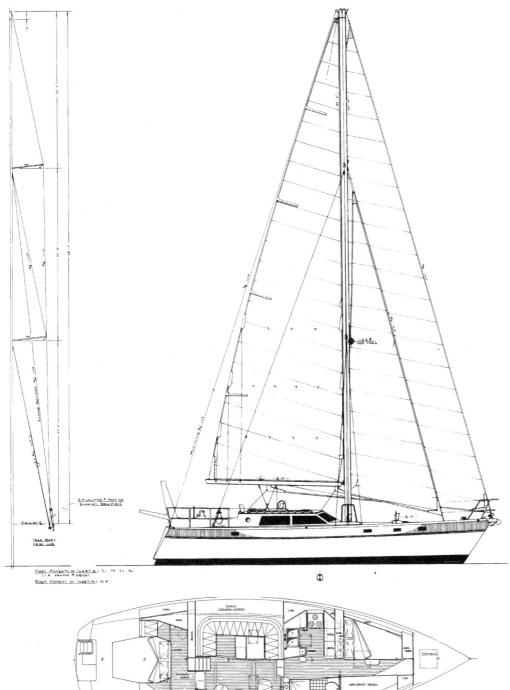

A PORTFOLIO OF BREWER DESIGNS

Design Number: 130
Name: **SOPHIA CHRISTINA**

LOA	46'1"
LWL	40'0'
Beam	13'5"
Draft	6'7"
Displacement	48,000 lbs.
Sail Area	1,354 sq. ft. 4 lowers; 1,752 sq. ft. full sail
Ballast	15,000 lbs.
Fuel	100 gals.
Water	150 gals.
Sail Area/Displ Ratio	16.4/21.2
Displ/Length Ratio	335

With her plumb bow and raking transom, *Sophia Christina* is styled after the large Boston pilot schooner *Lillie* of the gay '90s. Nevertheless, her accommodations are right up to modern standards and provide comfort, privacy, and convenience for long cruises. Berths for six to seven are fitted in three cabins and there is ample stowage throughout.

The rig sets generous sail area, and she is not a slouch in light air despite her full-keel profile. In stronger breezes the long waterline and powerful hull combine to assure good speeds under her four lowers. Her fine forward waterlines also assure that she will not be slowed by choppy seas either. On a beam reach *Sophia* can spread generous sail area and is a very exciting vessel to sail indeed. Still, she can be handled by a small crew as she sails nicely under just the foresail and jib in heavy weather.

Construction is traditional, with carvel planking over steam-bent frames and laid pine decks. Strip planking on bulkhead framing is also quite feasible.

The *Sophia Christina* has been licensed by the USCG for up to 14 passengers for day cruises and a normal complement for longer charters. She attracts attention wherever she goes, and she is husky enough that she can go anywhere.

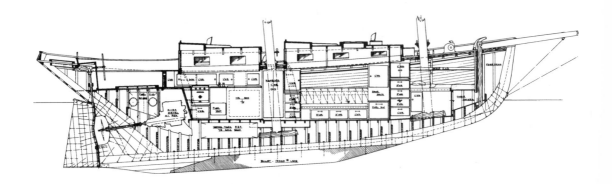

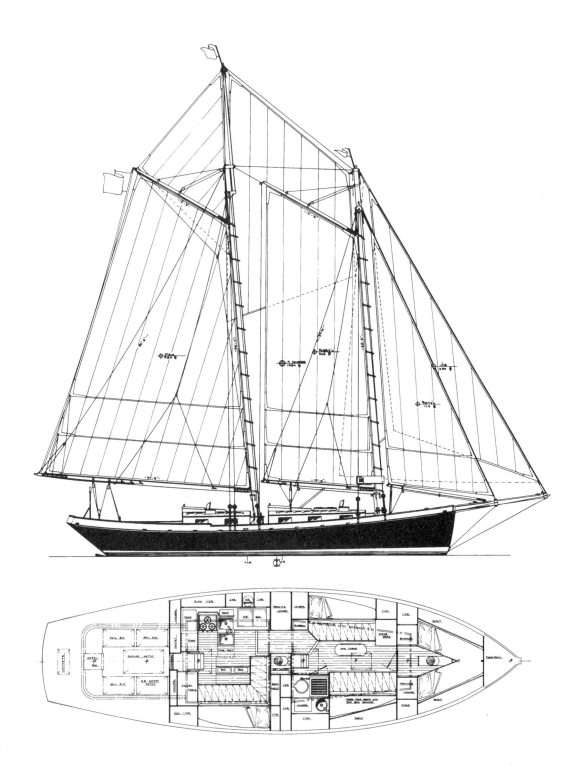

A PORTFOLIO OF BREWER DESIGNS

Design Number: 232
Name: *SANDINGO*

LOA	41'7"
LWL	35'0"
Beam	12'7"
Draft	5'6"
Displacement	25,000 lbs.
Sail Area	864 sq. ft.
Ballast	9,350 lbs.
Fuel	60 gals.
Water	120 gals.
Sail Area/Displ Ratio	16.2
Displ/Length Ratio	260.3

The general design of *Sandingo* was inspired by a 1991 article I wrote for *Cruising World* magazine as a result of its survey for the perfect 40-foot cruiser. *Sandingo's* owner saw the article and came to me to design his interpretation of it. This is the result.

The construction is of aluminum and the hull form is a typical radius-bilge shape pioneered by Brewer and Wallstrom in the mid-1970s. Similar hulls have been built by both amateurs and professionals all over North America and are well-proved in both service and resale value.

The accommodations provide four permanent berths and the dining settee can be converted to a double. The layout is not squeezed to jam in extra berths as are most production boats. Instead, the various spaces are large and will add to comfort afloat. The galley has extra good stowage and work space, the port settee is seven-and-a-half-feet long, the head contains a roomy stall shower, and the forward cabin has generous stowage in its nine-and-a-half-foot length.

The rig is similar to that of modern BOC racers, where the outer furling jib is a large reacher and downwind sail while the inner roller furler/reefer is a blade jib used for windward work. A detachable staysail stay is also fitted for a hanked-on storm jib. For normal weather conditions the crew does not need to go forward to change or reef.

Sandingo represents the ultimate in a fine, modern yacht in her size range. She offers strength, seaworthiness, comfort, and speed and could just be the ideal cruiser for the offshore family.

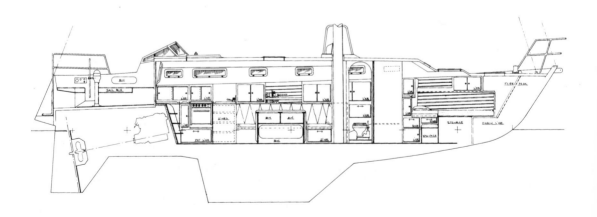

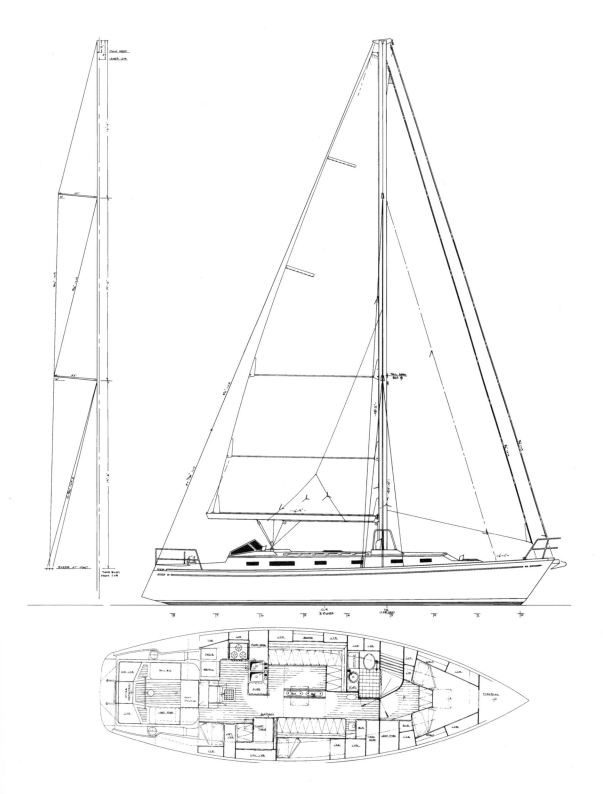

A PORTFOLIO OF BREWER DESIGNS

Design Number: 189
Name: **ARCTIC LOON**

LOA	59'7"
LWL	50'10"
Beam	16'1"
Draft	7'0"
Displacement	62,500 lbs.
Fuel	530 gals.
Water	250 gals.
Sail Area/Displ Ratio	16.95
Displ/Length Ratio	212.5

Arctic Loon was designed as a liveaboard retirement home and long range cruiser. Her accommodations provide a spacious owner's stateroom, two guest staterooms, and a single berth in the pilothouse. The galley is very complete, with space for a freezer, refrigerator, icemaker, trash compactor, and microwave oven. Supplies for extended voyages can be carried in the large walk-in pantry.

The hull form shows a powerful vessel with firm bilges, a fine entrance, and easy buttocks. With her low displacement/length ratio she will be easily driven and fast, yet her beamy hull will give her the stability to stand up well in a stiff breeze.

The rig is designed for ease of handling, with roller furling main, mizzen, and headsails. Electric winches provide power for jib sheeting and headsail furling. Sail area is generous for good performance in light air, and the inboard chainplates allow close sheeting for windward work.

Construction is of cored fiberglass for strength, lightness, and insulation. The large engine space provides room for an auxiliary generator, 600-g.p.d. water maker, large battery capacity, and a 115-b.h.p. diesel main engine along with other accessories.

There is no doubt that a yacht like *Arctic Loon* will provide her owner with a cruiser that can go anywhere in the world in comfort and safety.

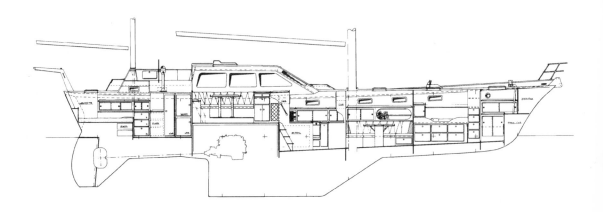

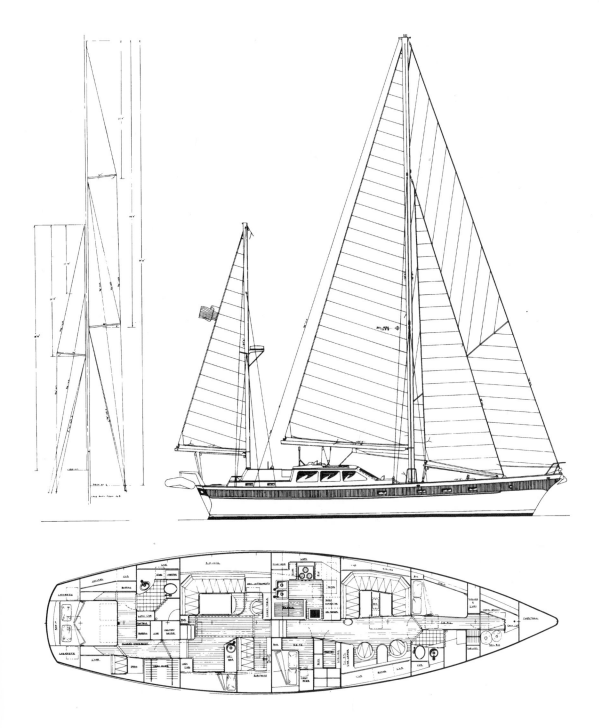

A PORTFOLIO OF BREWER DESIGNS

Design Number: 213
Name: **_TREE OF LIFE_**

LOA	69'0"
LWL	58'0"
Beam	18'11"
Draft	8'6'
Displacement	130,000 lbs.
Sail Area	2,585–3,894 sq, ft.
Ballast	27,500 lbs. lead
Fuel	500 gals.
Water	720 gals.
Sail Area/Displ Ratio	16.1/24.3
Displ/Length Ratio	297

Tree of Life was designed for an owner who is now living and cruising aboard her. _SAIL_ magazine honored me, her builder, and her owner by naming her one of the "100 Greatest Sailing Yachts in North America."

Construction is of heavy strip planking and laminated fir frames, all epoxy glued and coated. Decks are laid, oiled fir over plywood, and the entire vessel is very strong and durable thanks to modern wood construction techniques.

The accommodations provide berths for 10 in four separate cabins, plus a watch berth in the wheelhouse. Other features include a roomy owner's cabin, a library/office, a huge galley with dining counter and an 11-foot-long settee in the very spacious saloon.

The rig is quite traditional with its reefing topmasts, deadeyes, and fidded bowsprit. The sail plan sets very generous sail area though, and it moves her nicely, even in light breezes. Indeed, she was quite successful in a traditional schooner race off Nova Scotia, coming in first by almost five minutes.

A yacht such as _Tree of Life_ is not for everyone, obviously. Still, she would make a fine charter vessel as she has ample accommodations for a large crew and enough lines that everyone will keep busy. She is a beautiful sight surging along on a broad reach and a refreshing change from today's boring, flat-sheered, look-alike, blue-striped sloops. It was a great pleasure to design a yacht of this class.

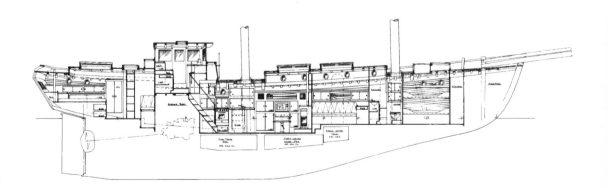

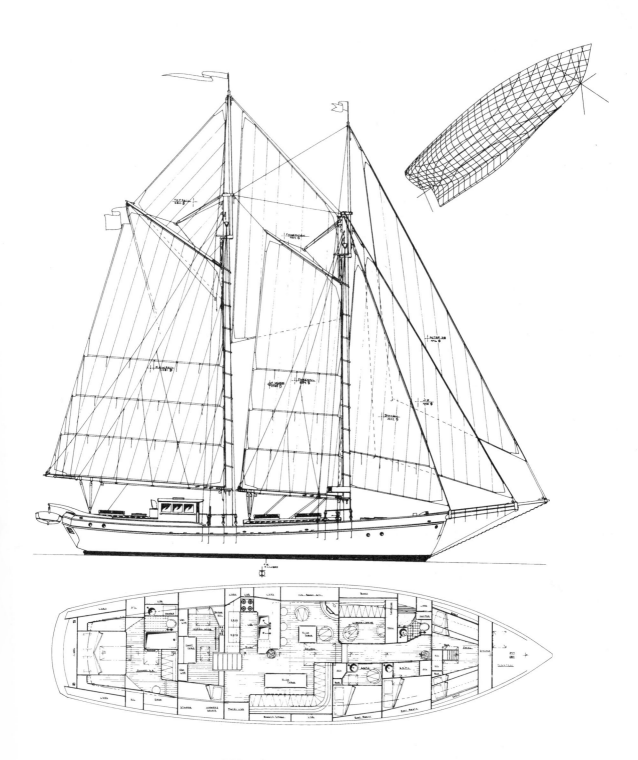

A PORTFOLIO OF BREWER DESIGNS

United States Coast Guard Auxiliary Courtesy Examination

The Coast Guard Auxiliary offers a Courtesy Marine Examination as a service to boat owners. While not a comprehensive survey, the examination helps the boat owner determine whether his boat is safe, and if not, what should be done to improve it. The following summary of the examination should help you run safety checks on your own boat.

A Courtesy Marine Examination cannot be performed while the boat is underway. Boats longer than 26 feet must be observed safely waterborne and moored. Boats of less than 26 feet in length and of known stock design can be examined out of the water, provided they are built of materials that are not subject to warping or shrinkage. All through-hull fittings on boats so examined must be properly installed in order for a decal to be awarded.

Use the following paragraphs as a check-off list to help you determine if your boat meets the requirements of federal law and the additional safety standards recommended by the auxiliary. Legal requirements are based upon the class of the motorboat or auxiliary-powered sailboat, which is in turn determined by its length. The length is measured in a straight line along the centerline from the foremost part of the boat to the aftermost part of the boat. Bowsprits, outboard motor brackets, and similar attachments are not included in this measurement.

Class A—less than 16 feet in length

Class 1—16 feet or over in length and less than 26 feet

Class 2—26 feet or over in length and less than 40 feet

Class 3—40 feet or over in length and not more than 65 feet

Numbering

Vessels equipped with propulsion machinery of any type are required to be numbered by the Coast Guard or by the state. In some states, boats not in this category must also be numbered. Check your state for its requirements.

The number must be properly displayed and the registration must be available for examination.

Natural Ventilation

All motorboats (including auxiliary sailboats) using gasoline or other fuel with a flash point less than 110° F., configured so that explosive or flammable vapors could be entrapped, must have at least two ventilator ducts fitted with cowls or the equivalent leading to each engine or fuel tank compartment for the efficient removal of explosive gases. The exhaust ducts shall lead from the lower portion of the bilge, and the intake ducts shall lead at least midway to the bilge below the carburetor air intake. Cowls shall be located and trimmed for maximum effectiveness and to prevent displaced fumes from being recirculated.

Classes A, 1, 2, and 3—required on all motorboats using fuel with a flash point less than 110° the construction or decking over of which was commenced after April 25, 1940.

Powered Ventilation

Vessels built after July 31, 1980, that have gasoline engines with a cranking motor (starter) for electrical generation, mechanical power, or propulsion in a closed compartment are required to have a powered ventilation system. This includes each compartment with such an engine.

No person may operate a vessel built after July 31, 1980, with a gasoline engine in a closed compartment unless it is equipped with an operable ventilation system that meets Coast Guard standards. The operator is required to keep the system in operating condition and ensure cowl and ducting are not blocked or torn.

Backfire Flame Control

Efficient means of backfire flame control is required for each carburetor on every inboard engine installed after April 25, 1940. Acceptable means of backfire flame control are:

- A Coast Guard-approved backfire flame arrestor secured to the air intake of each carburetor;
- or Engine and fuel intake system which provides equivalent protection and is labeled to indicate Coast Guard acceptance; or

- Any attachment firmly secured to the carburetor or arrangement of the air intake by means of which flames caused by backfire will be dispersed to the atmosphere in such a way as not to endanger the vessel or persons on board.

Fire Extinguishers

Fire extinguishers are classed according to their size and type. Extinguishers must bear Coast Guard and/or Underwriters Laboratory "Marine Type" approved labels. Type B fire extinguishers, designed for extinguishing flammable liquids, are required on motorboats. Equivalent sizes and extinguishing agent are shown on this table:

Minimum Number of Type B Fire Extinguishers Required

	FOAM	CARBON DIOXIDE	DRY CHEMICAL	HALON
Classification (min. lbs)	(min. gals) (type size)	(min. lbs)	(min. lbs)	(min. lbs)
B-I	1¼	4	2	2½
B-II	2½	15	10	None

Note: Carbon tetrachloride extinguishers and others of the toxic vaporizing-liquid type such as chlorobromomethane are no longer approved and are not accepted as required fire extinguishers.

The number of approved extinguishers required depends upon the class of the motorboat. One B-II extinguisher may be substituted for two B-I extinguishers. When the engine compartment of the motorboat is equipped with a fixed (built-in) extinguisher system, one less hand-portable B-I extinguisher is required.

Classes A and 1 outboard motorboats so constructed that entrapment of flammable vapors cannot occur are not required to carry fire extinguishers.

Classes A and 1 motorboats which do not meet the above exception and all Classes 2 and 3 motorboats must be equipped with fire extinguishers according to the following table:

Minimum Number of Hand-Portable Extinguishers Required

NO FIXED SYSTEM IN MACHINERY SPACE	FIXED FIRE EXTINGUISHING SYSTEM IN MACHINERY SPACE
Class A 1 B-I	None
Class 1 1 B-I	None
Class 2 2 B-I or 1 B-II	1 B-I
Class 3 3 B-I or 1 B-II and 1 B-I	2 B-I or 1 B-II

Bell, Whistle, or Horn

The requirement to carry a bell depends upon the class of boat. All bells must emit a clear bell-like tone when struck. The type of whistle or horn required differs with the class of boat. All horns or whistles must be capable of producing a blast of 2 seconds or more duration. The requirements for bell, whistle, or horn are shown in this table:

Bell	Whistle or Horn
Class A none required	None required (except where International Rules apply)
Class 1 none required	mouth-, hand- or power-operated, audible at least ½ mile
Class 2 required	hand- or power-operated, audible at least 1 mile
Class 3 required	power-operated, audible at least 1 mile

Note: While it is not required that all classes of boat carry the bell, whistle, or horn, the Rules of the Road require all vessels to give proper signals if a signaling situation develops.

Navigation Lights

All motorboats are required to display navigation lights prescribed for the class when operated between the hours of sunset and sunrise. The International configuration may be displayed on the high seas and on all United States waters. The Motorboat Act of 1940 configuration *cannot* be displayed on the high seas.

Lifesaving Devices

Every motorboat must have one approved lifesaving device in acceptable condition for each person on board or in tow (waterskier, surfboats, etc.). Lifesaving devices must be readily accessible. Kapok and fiberglass lifesaving devices that do not have plastic-covered buoyant pads are not acceptable.

- CLASSES 1, 2, and 3 motorboats must carry one approved Type I, II, or III PFD for each person on board and one Type IV PFD.
- CLASS A motorboats must carry an approved Type I, II, III, or IV PFD for each person on board.

Visual Distress Signals

All vessels used on coastal waters, the Great Lakes, territorial seas and those waters connected directly to them, up to a point where a body of water is less than two miles wide, must be equipped with visual distress signals. Vessels owned in the United States operating on the high seas must be equipped with visual distress signals. The following vessels are not required to carry day signals but must carry night signals when operating from sunset to sunrise.

- Recreational boats less than 16 feet in length.

- Boats participating in organized events such as races, regattas or marine parades.
- Open sailboats less than 26 feet in length not equipped with propulsion machinery.
- Manually propelled boats.

Pyrotechnic visual distress signals must be Coast Guard Approved, in serviceable condition and readily accessible. They are marked with a date showing the service life, which must not be expired. Launchers manufactured before January 1, 1982, intended for use with approved signals, are not required to be Coast Guard Approved. If pyrotechnic devices are selected, a minimum of three are required. That is three signals for day use and three signals for night. Some pyrotechnic signals meet both day and night use requirements. Pyrotechnic devices should be stored in a cool, dry location. A watertight container painted red or orange and prominently marked "DISTRESS SIGNALS" is recommended.

USCG Approved Pyrotechnic Visual Distress Signals and Associated Devices include:

- Pyrotechnic red flares, hand-held or aerial.
- Pyrotechnic orange smoke, hand-held or floating.
- Launchers for aerial red meteors or parachute flares.

Nonpyrotechnic visual distress signals must be in serviceable condition, readily accessible and certified by the manufacturer as complying with USCG requirements; they include:

- Orange distress flag
- Electric distress light

The distress flag is a day signal only. It must be at least 3 x 3 feet with a black square and ball on an orange background. It is most distinctive when attached and waved on a paddle or boathook or flown from a mast.

The electric distress light is accepted for night use only and must automatically flash the international SOS distress signal (...– – –...). This is an unmistakable distress signal. A standard flashlight is not acceptable as a visual distress signal.

Under Inland Navigation Rules, a high intensity white light flashing at regular intervals from 50 to 70 times per minute is considered a distress signal. Strobe lights used in inland waters shall only be used as a distress signal.

Regulations prohibit display of visual distress signals on the water under any circumstances except when assistance is required to prevent immediate or potential danger to persons on board a vessel.

All distress signals have distinct advantages and disadvantages; no single device is ideal under all conditions or suitable for all purposes. Pyrotechnics are excellent distress signals, universally recognized. However, there is potential for injury and property damage if not properly handled. These devices produce a very hot flame; the residue can cause burns and ignite flammable material. Pistol-launched and handheld parachute flares and meteors have many characteristics of a firearm and must be handled with caution.

Auxiliary Standards for Award of Decal

Before a boat can be awarded the Courtesy Marine Examination decal, it must meet all the foregoing requirements of the federal law, and in addition it must meet the following standards considered necessary for safe operation:

- *Lifesaving devices.* There must be at least as many approved lifesaving devices of the type required for the class of boat as there are berths. A boat with fewer than two bunks must have at least two approved lifesaving devices aboard. Lifesaving devices must be readily accessible.

- *Fire extinguishers.* All Class A and Class 1 motor-boats, whether or not they are equipped with a fixed fire extinguishing system, must carry one hand-portable fire extinguisher of approved type.
- *Navigation lights* must be of a configuration specified for the class of boat and must be operative and fully visible through the required arc.
- *Distress Signals.* Recreational boats 16 feet or longer (with a few exceptions) must carry distress signals (see above).
- *Galley stove.* If carried, the galley stove must be securely mounted so that it cannot shift position. Stoves must be installed so that no flammable materials in the vicinity can be ignited. Any of the common types of fuel may be used except gasoline.
- Permanently installed *fuel tanks* must be securely mounted so that they cannot shift position.
- *Fuel tank vent.* A vent terminating outboard of the hull and compartments must lead to each permanently installed fuel tank.
- A *fuel tank fill pipe* leading to permanently installed fuel tanks must fit into a filling plate located on deck outside the cockpit to ensure that spilled fuel flows overboard.
- *Portable fuel tanks and spare fuel containers.* Tanks and containers that exceed 7 gallons are not classed as portable tanks, and must meet all requirements for permanently installed tanks. Tanks and spare fuel containers of less than 7 gallons must be tight and sufficiently sturdy to withstand ordinary usage. Glass or other breakable materials may not be used for portable fuel tanks or containers.
- *Carburetor drip pan.* A drip pan must be installed under all side-draft or up-draft carburetors not provided with a effective sump.
- *Backfire flame control.* All inboard motorboats, regardless of date of construction or engine installation, must meet current federal requirements for backfire flame control.
- *Whistle or sound producing device.* All Class A boats must carry a whistle or sound-producing device capable of producing a blast of 2 seconds or more duration and audible at least ½ mile.
- *Ventilation.* All motorboats regardless of class or date of construction must meet the current federal requirements for ventilation.
- *Electrical installation.* Wiring must be in good condition and properly installed. There should be no open knife switches located in the bilge.
- *Anchor and anchor line.* The boat must be equipped with an adequate anchor and line of suitable size and length for the locality.
- *General condition.* The vessel must be in good overall condition, the hull sound, fuel lines intact and properly installed. The decal will not be awarded to a vessel that is not generally ship-shape and in seaworthy condition.

Class A motorboats must carry the following additional equipment.

- Pump or bailer
- Paddle or oar
- Distress signals (when operating at night)

Recommended Condition and Equipment Standards

While not cause of withholding the decal, the Auxiliary recommends the following standards of condition and equipment. Your boating pleasure depends upon the condition of your craft and how you outfit and maintain her.

- Through-hull fittings should have shut-off valves or wooden plugs accessible for use.
- Fuel lines should lead from the top of the tank and be equipped with shut-off valves at the tank and engine.

- Auxiliary generators should have separate fuel tanks.
- All switches located in the bilges should be designed for submerged use.
- Distress signaling equipment should be carried on every boat.
- A manual bilge pump should be carried on every boat irrespective of any mechanical pumping devices.
- Handrails should be secured with through bolts.
- Spare canisters should be carried for horns or whistles that operate from compressed gas.
- Spare batteries and spare bulbs should be carried for battery-operated lights.
- A fully equipped first-aid kit should be carried in every boat.
- Have tools and spare parts on board in usable condition.
- The safe loading plate affixed at the time of manufacture should be legible, and the load capacities indicated thereon should not be exceeded.

APPENDIX C

Suggested Reading

Books

Buehler, George. *Buehler's Backyard Boatbuilding*. Camden, ME: International Marine Publishing, 1990.

Chapelle, Howard I. *Boatbuilding*. New York: W. W. Norton & Company, 1941.

___. Yacht *Designing and Planning, Revised Edition*. New York: W. W. Norton & Company, 1971.

___. *American Small Sailing Craft*. New York: W. W. Norton & Company, 1951.

Colvin, Thomas. *Steel Boatbuilding, From Plans to Launching*. Camden, ME: International Marine Publishing, 1992.

Culler, R.D. *Skiffs and Schooners*. Camden, ME: International Marine Publishing, 1990.

Devlin, Samual. *Devlin's Boatbuilding*. Camden, ME: International Marine Publishing, 1994.

Gardner, John. *The Dory Book*. Mystic, CT: Mystic Seaport Museum, Inc., 1987.

—-. *Building Classic Small Craft, Vol. I*. Camden, ME: International Marine Publishing, 1991.

—-. *More Building Classic Small Craft*. Camden, ME: International Marine Publishing, 1990.

Gerr, Dave. *The Nature of Boats: Insights and Esoterica for the Nautically Obsessed*. Camden, ME:

International Marine Publishing, 1992.

Guzzwell, John. *Modern Wooden Yacht Construction*. Camden, ME: International Marine Publishing, 1979. (out of print)

Hankinson, Ken. *Fiberglass Boat Building for Amateurs*. Bellflower, CA: Glen-L. Marine Designs, 1982.

Henderson, Richard. *Fifty-Three Boats You Can Build*. Camden, ME: International Marine Publishing, 1987. (out of print)

Herreshoff, L. Francis. *Sensible Cruising Designs*. Camden, ME: International Marine Publishing, 1991.

Kinney, Francis S. *Skene's Elements of Yacht Design*. New York: G. P. Putnam's Sons, 1973. (out of print)

Klingel, Gilbert. *Boatbuilding with Steel*, Revised by Thomas Colvin. Camden, ME: International Marine Publishing, 1990.

Leather, John. *Clinker Boatbuilding*. Dobbs Ferry, NY: Sheridan House, Inc., 1987.

McIntosh, David C. *How to Build a Wooden Boat*. Brooklin, ME: WoodenBoat Publications, 1988.

Parker, Reuel B. *The New Cold-Molded Boatbuilding: From Lofting to Launching*. Camden, ME: International Marine Publishing, 1992.

Pollard, Stephen. *Boatbuilding with Aluminum*. Camden, ME: International Marine, 1993.

Rabl, S.S. *Boatbuilding in Your Own Backyard*. Centreville, MD: Cornell Maritime Press, 1958.

Spurr, Daniel. *Yacht Style*. Camden, ME: International Marine Publishing, 1990.

Steward, Robert. *Boatbuilding Manual, Fourth Edition*. Camden, ME: International Marine Publishing Co, 1994.

Taylor, Roger C. *Thirty Classic Boat Designs*. Camden, ME: International Marine Publishing, 1992.

Thomas, Barry. *Thirty Wooden Boats: A Second Catalog of Building Plans*. Brooklin, ME: WoodenBoat Publications, 1988.

Vaitses, Alan. *Lofting*. Camden ME: International Marine Publishing, 1980. (out of print)

Periodicals

Boatbuilder, P.O. Box 540638, Merritt Island, FL 32954.

Cruising World, 5 John Clarke Road, Newport, RI 02840.

Messing About in Boats, 29 Burley Street, Wenham, MA 01984.

Motor Boating & Sailing, 224 West 57th Street, New York, NY 10019.

SAIL, 275 Washington Street, Newton, MA 02158-1630.

Sailing, 125 E. Main Street, Port Washington, WI 53074.

WoodenBoat, P.O. Box 78, Brooklin, ME 04616.

A Short Glossary

Aback: With the wind on the wrong side of the sails.

Abaft: Behind an object in relation to the bow, i.e., "abaft the mast" means "behind the mast."

Abeam: At a right angle to the line of the keel, off the beam.

Aft: Toward the stern.

After body: The aft section of the vessel.

Alee: Downwind, to the leeward side.

Aloft: Above the deck.

Amidships (also **midships**): The center of the vessel; may refer to either fore and aft or athwartship direction.

Anchor light (also **riding light**): A white light visible in a 360-degree circle, often fitted at the masthead.

Apparent wind: The wind direction that is felt on a moving vessel. It differs from the true wind due to the vessel's speed and course.

Astern: Abaft the vessel.

Athwartships: At a right angle to the centerline of the vessel.

Auxiliary: A vessel propelled by both sails and engine, separately or together; also the engine in an auxiliary yacht.

Back: The wind backs when it changes direction to the left.

Backstay: The part of the rigging that supports the mast from the aft part of the vessel.

Balanced rudder: One that carries 10% or so of its area forward of its pivot point.

Ballast: Weight (iron, lead, rocks, etc.) carried low in a vessel to increase stability.

Battens: Light wood or plastic strips fitted to support the aft end of a sail. These fit into pockets sewn in the sail.

Beam: The maximum width of the vessel; also an athwartship member supporting the deck or cabin roof.

Beamy: A wide vessel.

Beat: To sail to windward on alternate tacks.

Bed: The support for the engine or other heavy equipment.

Berth: A narrow, hard, wet place in which one sleeps aboard a boat.

Bilge: The turn of the hull between the topsides and bottom; also the dank, smelly place above the keel where the oily water collects.

Binnacle: The box or hood containing the compass.

Bitts: Vertical posts of wood or metal for mooring or towing line attachment.

Bobstay: Chain or wire rigging running from the stem to the bowsprit end. For 10% of its life it supports the bowsprit; the other 90% it spends sawing at the mooring line.

Boom: The spar to which the foot of a fore-and-aft sail is attached.

Boomkin: A spar extending abaft the vessel to support a permanent backstay or for sheeting a sail.

Bow: The forward end of a vessel.

Bowsprit: A spar extending forward of the bow from which jibs are set.

Brightwork: Varnished wood surface.

Bulb keel: A sailboat fin with a streamlined bulb of iron or lead at the lower end, designed to increase stability.

Bulkhead: A vertical partition that forms the "wall" of a compartment.

Bulwark: The extension of the planking above the deck to form a rail.

Bury: The part of a mast below the deck or cabin roof.

By the lee: Sailing downwind with the wind and main boom on the same side of the vessel. It can be dangerous.

Camber: The athwartships curve of a vessel's deck.

Caulking: The oakum or cotton strands driven into the seams of a wood vessel to make it watertight, pronounced corking.

Centerboard: A device lowered through the hull to increase lateral area in order to decrease leeway.

Chainplates: The fittings on the hull that accept the lower end of the shrouds in order to support the mast.

Cheek block: A block with one side fastened to a spar or deck.

Chine: The corner between the topsides and the bottom of a flat or V-bottom hull.

Clew: The lower aft corner of a sail.

Clipper bow: The bow shape reminiscent of clipper ships, with a graceful reverse S curve.

Close hauled: Sailing to windward with the sails trimmed in as close to midships as possible.

Close winded: A boat that sails well to windward. Weatherly is another term used to describe this desirable feature.

Club: The boom on a jib or staysail. i.e., club jib.

Coaming: The raised sides of the cockpit; also, the side of a trunk cabin.

Collision bulkhead: A watertight bulkhead just abaft the bow.

Come about (also **tack**): To change tacks by bringing the bow through the eye of the wind.

Companionway: The access to the interior of the yacht from the cockpit. A favorite place to sit or stand, unfortunately!

Covering board: The outermost deck plank, covering the top of the frames.

Cruiser stern: A rounded stern with moderate overhang.

Cutwater: The leading edge of the stem.

Deadlight: Fixed glass ports; also the metal plate that closes off a broken portlight in an emergency.

Deadwood: Heavy timbers at the stern of a vessel connecting the keel to the ballast or sternpost.

Dorade ventilator: A self-draining ventilator.

Double-ender: A sharp-sterned hull.

Downhaul: A line or tackle used to pull down a sail or spar.

Draft: The depth of water required to float a vessel.

Drag: Another term for resistance; also, a keel that increases its draft toward the aft end is said to have drag.

Eddy: Water or air currents moving in confused, circular patterns.

Entrance: The vessel's bow at and just above the waterline.

Factor of safety: The relationship of the ultimate strength of a material or item to the working loads it will undergo.

Fair: Used to describe a hull without distortions, humps, or hollows.

Fairlead: An eye of plastic or wood used to lead lines in the desired direction.

Feathering Propeller: A propeller in which the blades turn to line up with the flow of the water when the boat is sailing.

Fiddle black: A block with 2 sheaves in line.

Fiddle: A rail used to keep items in place in heavy seas; often mistakenly called a sea rail.

Fin keel: A deep fin, separate from the rudder, to provide lateral resistance to a sailboat hull. It is not actually a keel.

Fisherman staysail: A four sided sail set high between the masts of schooners. Its head runs between the masts.

Flush deck: The deck line from the bow to abaft the mast is not broken by a cabin.

Foot: The lower edge of a sail.

Fore and aft: Along the line of the keel.

Foremast: The forward mast of a schooner.

Forepeak: The stowage compartment in the bow of a vessel.

Foresail: The sail set abaft the foremast of a schooner.

Forefoot: Where the keel meets the stem.

Frame: An athwartship structural member of a vessel supporting the planking or plating. The uninitiated often call it a rib.

Freeing port: An opening in the bulwarks to drain water off the deck.

Freeboard: The distance from the water to the deck edge.

Full and by: Sailing as close to the wind as possible with all sails drawing.

Gaff: The spar along the head of a gaff sail.

Gale: A storm with a wind speed of 34 to 40 knots.

Galley: The cooking compartment of a vessel.

Gallows frame: A frame rising above the deck or cabin that is used to support the boom.

Gammoning: The lashing securing the bowsprit to the stemhead. A gammoning iron is a metal fitting serving the same purpose.

Garboard strake: The plank on a wood vessel that fastens to the keel; the lowest plank.

Garvey: A scow-type vessel developed on Barnegat Bay.

Gasket: Rope or Dacron ties used to secure the sail to the boom when the sail is lowered.

Genoa (also jenny): A large jib that overlaps the mast.

Gimbals: A pivot device used to keep stoves, compasses, etc., level when the vessel heels.

Gooseneck: The metal fitting securing the boom to the mast.

Goosewing jibe: A bad jibe that results in the boom and gaff ending up on opposite sides of the mast.

Ground tackle: The anchor, chain, rode, etc.

Gudgeon: Eyes set in the stern or rudderpost to accept the rudder pintles and permit the rudder to swing.

Gunkholing: Cruising in shoal water and overnighting in small coves.

Gunter rig: A jibheaded rig in which the upper part of the mainsail is supported by a vertically sliding gaff.

Gunwale: The rail of the boat, pronounced gunnel.

Gybe (also jibe): Changing tack by passing the wind over the stern.

Gypsy: The drum of a windlass or capstan.

Halyards (also halliards): Lines used to hoist sails.

Hand rail: Wood or metal hand hold, usually fitted on the cabin top.

Hanks: Fittings sewn on the jibs for fastening the sails to the stays.

Hard-a-lee: The command to put the helm over to come about.

Hard over: To put the helm over in either direction as far as possible.

Hauling part: The part of a tackle that is pulled upon, the other end being the standing part.

Head: The toilet; also the toilet compartment. Also the upper side of a gaff sail or the upper corner of a Bermudan sail.

Headboard: The wood or metal fitting sewn into the head of a Bermudan sail.

Headsail: A staysail or jib set forward of the fore or main mast.

Headstay: The stay running from the masthead to the stemhead, or bowsprit end if fitted.

Heave to: To bring a sailboat's head to wind so that she will stay there. The purpose is to hold the general position when riding out a gale.

Heel: The lower part of the mast or of a rudder; also the athwartship

inclination of the vessel.

Heeling arm: The vertical distance between the center of effort of the sails and the center of lateral resistance of the hull.

Helm: The tiller or steering wheel.

Helm's alee: A warning sounded by the helmsman when tacking, in order to brace the crew to their duties.

Hiking: To get the crew weight to windward outside the rail to increase stability.

Hogged: A condition in an older wood vessel where the ends have drooped.

Hood ends: On a wood vessel, the ends of the planks that are set into the rabbet in the stem and sternpost.

Hoops: Rings of wood or plastic that hold a gaff sail to the mast.

Horn timber: In wood vessels, the timber extending aft on the centerline from the rudder post to the transom.

Horsepower: A unit of power equal to lifting a weight of 550 pounds one foot in one second.

Inboard: Toward the centerline of the vessel.

Irish pennant: A loose line dangling in the rigging.

Jaws: The fitting of a gaff rig holding the boom and gaff to the mast.

Jib: A triangular sail set forward of the fore or mainmast.

Jib netting: A rope network below the bowsprit to keep the jib and crew from falling into the sea.

Jibstay: See **Headstay**.

Jib topsail: A light-weather jib set

high on the headstay of a double-headsail rig.

Jiffy reef: A form of slab reefing arranged so that the sail can be reefed quickly.

Jigger: A term for a small mizzen sail on a yawl or ketch.

Jury rig: An emergency rig set up when dismasted; any gear rigged to carry out the job of a broken part.

Kedging: Moving the vessel by heaving on a rode attached to an anchor that has been carried out by a dinghy.

Keel: The backbone of a vessel to which the floors and frames are fastened.

Keelson: A longitudinal member fitted on top of the floors to add strength to the keel.

Knees: Triangular-shaped wood or metal plates fitted to strengthen the vessel.

Knot: One nautical mile per hour. A nautical mile = 1.151 land miles.

Lazarette: A storage compartment in the stern of a vessel.

Lazyjacks: Light lines running from mast to boom to form a simple netting to hold the lowered sail.

Leech: The aft side of a fore-and-aft sail; the edges of a squaresail.

Lee: Downwind, away from the wind.

Leeward: Downwind.

Leeway: The drift of a sailboat to leeward due to the force of the wind on the sails.

Left-hand propeller: One that turns counterclockwise when viewed from astern.

Limber: A drain hole through the

floors and frames that allows water to flow to the bilge pump.

Longitudinals (also **stringers**): Framing that runs fore and aft.

Loose-footed: A fore-and-aft sail that is not attached to a boom.

Luff: The leading edge of a fore and aft sail. To luff is to allow the vessel to come head-to-wind so that wind pressure on the leading edge of the sail is relieved.

Mainmast: The forward mast of yawls and ketches; the aft mast of a two-masted schooner.

Mainsail: The sail set from the mainmast.

Margin plank: The plank around the cabin trunk and hatches into which the deck planks are nibbed.

Mast coat: The canvas or neoprene fitted around the mast at the deck, to keep water from getting below. (It is to laugh!)

Mast partners: In a wood yacht, the structural members reinforcing the deck or cabin roof at the mast.

Mast step: The structural member that supports the heel of the mast.

Mast wedges: Wood or hard rubber wedges driven between the mast and the partners.

Midships: The fore-and-aft center of the vessel.

Mizzenmast: The aft mast of a yawl or ketch. See **Jigger**.

Mizzen: The sail set abaft the mizzenmast.

Mizzen staysail: A light, triangular sail set flying from the mizzenmast head and sheeted to the mizzen boom end.

Mule: A triangular sail set from the

main backstay of a ketch or yawl and sheeted to the mizzenmast head.

Near gale: Storm with winds of 28 to 33 knots.

North River jibe: Jibing quickly without first hauling in the mainsheet. It can be dangerous.

Oakum: Tarred rope fibers used for caulking.

Off the wind: To sail downwind.

Offing: Well out to sea but with land in sight.

On the beam: At a right angle to the line of the keel.

On the bow: 45 degrees or less from the bow.

On the quarter: 45 degrees or less from the stern.

On the wind: Close hauled.

Outpoint: To sail closer to the wind than a rival vessel.

Out of trim: To be floating down by the bow or stern, or with an athwartship list.

Outboard: Outside the hull of the vessel; also, a portable motor.

Outfoot: To sail faster than a rival yacht.

Outhaul: A line or fitting used to haul out the clew of a sail.

Over rigged: Rigging heavier than necessary.

Oversparred: Carrying more sail than stability warrants; mast too lofty or boom too long.

Overboard: Over the side, in the water.

Overhang: The projection of the bow or stern beyond the waterline endings.

Painter: The towing line made fast to the bow of a dinghy.

Parrel: The wire or line holding the gaws of a gaff or boom to the mast.

Part: One section of a rope or tackle; also, to break.

Patent log: A distance-measuring device.

Pay: To fill the seam in a deck with pitch or seam compound. The devil seam is the outer seam in the deck, and "The devil to pay and no pitch hot" is an old seafaring term.

Pay off: To turn the bow away from the wind.

Peak: The upper aft corner of a gaff sail. Also the end of the gaff. Also a compartment in the ends of the vessel.

Pelican hook: A form of slip hook used on lifeline gates.

Pinrail: A rail with holes to accept belaying pins.

Pinch: To point a sailing vessel slightly too high to windward, causing the sails to luff.

Pintle: The pin that fits into the gudgeon to form a support and hinge for the rudder.

Pitch: The falling and rising of a vessel in a fore and aft direction; also the distance the propeller would move forward in one revolution if it were threading into solid material. A material used to pay deck seams.

Pitch pole: A disaster in which a breaking sea causes a vessel to cartwheel her stern over her bow.

Plain sail: The working sails.

Plow: Another name for the CQR anchor.

Poop: The raised deck at the stern

of some vessels.

Pooped: Having a sea break over the stern.

Port: The left-hand side of the vessel when looking forward; also an opening in the side of the vessel; gun port, portlight.

Port tack: Sailing with the wind coming over the port side.

Preventer: A line running forward from the boom to prevent an accidental jibe.

Pulpit: The tubular metal railing at the bow or stern.

Quadrant: The fitting on the rudder stock to which the steering cables attach. It is a quarter of a circle.

Quarter: The side of the vessel abaft the beam and forward of the stern; in effect, the aft "corner."

Rabbet: The groove cut in the stem, stern, and keel of a wood vessel to accept the planking.

Rail: The top of the bulwarks.

Rake: The angle of the masts or deck structures.

Ratlines: Rope rungs seized to the shrouds to form a ladder.

Reach: To sail on a course between close hauled and running free. Close reach—wind forward of the beam. Beam reach—wind abeam. Broad reach—wind on the quarter.

Ready about: The order given to make ready to tack the vessel.

Reduction gear: The gearbox that reduces engine RPMs to workable propeller RPMs.

Reef: To reduce sail area. Close reefed—sail reduced to the last set of reef points.

Reef cringle: A grommet or eye in the luff and leach of a sail at the ends of the reef.

Reef points: Short lengths of line attached to the sail at intervals to secure the foot of the sail when reefed.

Reef tackle: The line that pulls the reef cringles down to the boom.

Ribband: A strip of wood used to support and fair the frames in wood-boat construction.

Rig: A vessel's arrangement of masts and sails; also, to set up the masts and rigging in a vessel.

Rigging: The wires and ropes that support the masts (standing rigging) and hoist and trim the sails and spars (running rigging).

Right: To return to upright, as to right a capsized boat.

Right-handed propeller: One which turns clockwise when viewed from astern.

Roach: The curve in the leach of a sail or the foot of a genoa.

Rode: The anchor line; often anchor rode.

Roll: Side-to-side oscillation of a vessel.

Roller furling gear: The sail rolls up on a wire luff or aluminum foil; common on headsails and now on mainsails either inside or outside the mast.

Roller-reefing gear: A method of reefing by rolling the sail around the boom; now obsolete.

Rose box: The strainer at the bottom of the hose leading to the bilge pump; also strum box.

Rudder irons: The pintles and

gudgeons.

Rudderpost: The structural member that supports the rudder on a wood or metal vessel.

Rudder port: The tube through which the rudder stock enters the vessel.

Rudder stock: The metal rod or tube to which the rudder is attached. May be of wood on older or large vessels.

Run: To sail downwind; also the hull of the vessel underwater toward the stern.

Running backstays (also **runners**): Temporary backstays set up to tension the jib or staysail luff. The weather runner is set up.

Running lights: Lights carried when underway at night.

Samson post: A single bitt; see **Bitts**.

Scandalize: To reduce sail on a gaff-rigged vessel by letting go the peak halyard.

Scantlings: The dimensions of the structural parts of a vessel.

Scend: The lifting of a vessel on a swell or passing sea.

Screw: Another term for propeller.

Scud: To run before a gale with storm sails or no sails. Also driving mists or broken clouds moving fast under nimbus clouds.

Scuppers: Drains on deck or in the cockpit to carry water overboard.

Sea chest: The intake between the hull and the seacock.

Seacock: A valve connecting a vessel's piping to sea water.

Sea water: Weighs 64 pounds per cubic foot; 35 cu. ft. weigh 2240 pounds or one long ton.

Seaworthy: A vessel that is well designed, built, and equipped and in good condition to proceed to sea.

Seize: Binding two ropes together with light line or marline.

Set: The direction of the current; the direction in which a vessel is moved by the tide and/or wind.

Shackle: A horseshoe-shaped metal fitting with a bolt or pin across the open end.

Shaft: The rod connecting the engine to the propeller.

Sheer: The curve of the deck line viewed from the side.

Sheet: The line attached to the boom or to the clew of a loose-footed sail in order to trim the sail. It is not a sail!

Shipshape: Everything in its place.

Shiver: The luff of the sail shaking from pointing too high.

Shoot: To luff a sailboat and move to windward by the vessel's momentum.

Short board: A short tack.

Shorten sail: To reduce sail by reefing or taking down sail.

Shrouds: The wires supporting a mast athwartships.

Shutter: The last plank fitted when building a wooden vessel.

Side lights: The port (red) and starboard (green) running lights.

Siding: The thickness of a timber. Molding is the dimension to which the timber is cut.

Skeg: The extension of the hull forward of and supporting the rudder.

Slab reefing: Reefing by lowering sail to a line of reef points parallel to the foot.

Snatch block: A block that can open to allow the line to be placed in it, rather than having to pull the whole length through.

Sole: The cabin floor.

Spade rudder: A rudder supported only by the strength of its rudder stock, unsupported by the hull or a skeg.

Spars: A general term for the mast, boom, gaff, spinnaker pole, etc.

Spinnaker: A large, light triangular headsail used for reaching and running; set with its tack held out by a spinnaker pole.

Spreaders: Wood or metal struts used to spread the shrouds to a better staying angle.

Spring stay: The stay between the mastheads of a schooner.

Squatting: The sinking of the stern due to excess speed.

Stability: The moment or force that returns a heeled vessel to upright.

Stanchions: Upright support posts. Lifeline stanchions are often meant.

Standing part: The part of a rope or tackle that is made fast to an eye or block.

Starboard: The right side of the vessel when looking forward.

Starboard tack: Sailing with the wind coming over the starboard side.

Start: To ease off on a line.

Stay: The wire rigging that supports a mast in a fore-and-aft position, i.e., headstay, backstay, staysail stay.

Staysail: The triangular sail set on the staysail stay or forestay.

Stem: The timber or metal bar supporting the planking at the bow above the keel, or that part of the hull between the waterline and the deck.

Step: To step a mast is to set it in the vessel.

Stern: The after part of a vessel.

Sternpost: The structural member between the keel and horn timber.

Stern tube: The tube through which the shaft runs.

Stopwater: In a wood boat, a dowel driven at a joint to prevent water seepage.

Storm: Officially, wind speeds of 48 to 55 knots.

Storm sails: Small sails of heavy material intended for use in heavy winds.

Stowage: An area where items are stored.

Strake: A line of planking or plating running the length of the vessel.

Stringer: A fore and aft structural member, i.e., bilge stringer.

Strong gale: A storm with wind speeds of 41 to 47 knots.

Strut: The appendage that supports the propeller shaft.

Stuffing box: A device to prevent water entry around a shaft or rudder stock.

Swaging: A terminal fused to the end of wire rigging.

Swamped: A boat awash in water.

Tabernacle: A structure on deck that supports the mast and allows it to be hinged for lowering.

Tack: The forward lower corner of a sail; also, a course sailed with the wind on one side of the yacht. To tack is to change course by bringing the wind across the bow.

Tackle: A purchase composed of rope and blocks to increase power. It is pronounced taykle.

Tangs: Metal fittings that attach the rigging to the mast.

Telltale: A light ribbon tied to the rigging to indicate wind direction.

Telltale compass: A compass suspended over the captain's berth so he can check the course without going on deck.

Thimble: A ring with grooved edges to accept a wire or rope.

Thole pins: Wood pins set in the rail of a rowboat to retain the oars.

Throat: The forward upper corner of a gaff sail; that part of the gaff nearest the mast.

Tiller: A wood or metal bar connected to the rudder to steer the vessel.

Tiller ropes: Lines leading from the tiller or quadrant to the steering wheel.

Tip clearance: The distance by which a propeller blade clears the hull.

Toe rail: A low rail along the deck edge.

Topmast: The mast next above the lower mast on a gaff-rigged vessel.

Topping lift: The line running from the mast to the boom to support the boom when the sail is lowered.

Topsail: The sail above the mainsail on a gaff-rigged vessel.

Topsides: The area of the hull between the deck and the bottom paint. It is not the deck and cabin!

Transom: The stern of a square sterned vessel.

Traveller: The track with car, or the athwartship rod, to which a boom is sheeted. A bridle is a wire traveller.

Treenail: A wood pin used as fastenings on a wooden vessel in place of metal (now obsolete); pronounced trunnel.

Trice: Haul up.

Trick: Time spent at the helm.

Trim: The fore-and-aft flotation of a vessel. Trimmed by the head means trimmed down by the bow.

Trunk cabin: A cabin raised above the main deck.

Trysail: A storm sail set in place of the mainsail.

Tuck: The part of the hull where the bottom meets the keel or fin.

Turn of the bilge: The part of the hull where the topsides turn to form the bottom.

Two blocked: A tackle set up so completely that the blocks meet.

Underfoot: The anchor is on the bottom and the rode is straight up and down. Also up and down.

Underway: The vessel has cast off from the pier and has her anchor up, whether moving or not.

Vangs: Lines used to control and trim a gaff. Boom vang is a tackle that hauls down the boom to flatten the mainsail.

Veer: To pay out anchor line; also, for the wind to change direction to the right.

Wake: The disturbed water behind

a vessel.

Wale: A heavy strake running fore and aft below the sheer.

Wall-sided: A vessel with flat, vertical topsides.

Waterplane: The shape of the hull at the waterline.

Weather: Toward the wind; the windward side.

Weather cloths: Canvas panels laced on the aft lifelines to protect against wind and spray.

Weatherly: A vessel that sails well to windward.

Web frame: An extra-deep frame fitted at stress areas in the vessel.

Weeping: A slow, steady leak.

Weigh: Raise anchor.

Wheel: The steering wheel; also the propeller.

Whisker pole: A spar used to hold out the clew of a headsail when running.

Wide berth: A safe distance from another boat, a shoal, or the land.

Winch: A mechanical device for increasing power when hauling on running rigging.

Wind sail: A cloth air scoop to ventilate a vessel.

Windlass: A mechanical device for hoisting an anchor.

Windward: The direction from which the wind is blowing.

Wing and wing: To sail downwind with sails on opposite sides of the vessel.

Working sails: Those sails that are regularly used, excluding light and storm sails.

Working to windward: To tack to windward.

Index

A

Accommodation layout, 70-77, 97
Aesthetics, 62-69
Amas, 20
American Boat and Yacht Council, 80
America's Cup, 32
Anchor, 132
    storage for, 75
Architect, naval, 99

B

Backfire flame control, 129, 132
Backstays, 49
Ballast, 16, 47, 97
Barnacles, 43, 89
Beam, 3, 24-26
    LWL ratios, 25, 26
Beam WL, 3
Bells, 130
Berths, 70
Bilge boards, 43-45
Blisters, fiberglass resin, 92
Boatbuilder magazine, 99
Boatbuilding, amateur, 102-04
Body plan, 21, 24-32
Bonding, electrical, 85
Books (suggested reading), 134-35
Bow shape, 63-65
    clipper, 63, 65
    plumb, 63, 65
    raked, 65, 65
    spoon, 63-65
    tumblehome, 63, 65

Bow thruster, 60
Box scow, 9
"Brewer bite," 40
Brewer designs, portfolio of, 105-27
Bugeye, 68
Bunks, *see* Berths
Buttocks, 22, 23, 34
    quarter, 34
Butts, 85, 86

C

Cabin shape, 67-68
CAD (computer-aided design) programs, 24, 37
Carvel, 82
Catboat, 53-54, 63, 68, 105
    Cape Cod, design of, 105-07
Catches, magnetic, 77
Centerboarder, 40, 42-43
Center of buoyancy (CB), 3, 5
Center of effort, 6-7, 56-57
Center of flotation (CF), 3
Center of gravity, 32
Center of lateral plane (CLP), 6, 56-57
Character boats, 68-69
Chines, 12, 21
Clencher, 81
Clinker, 81
Coast Guard regulations, 80
    Courtesy Examination, 128-33
Cockpits, self-bailing, 79
Cod's-head and mackerel-tail, 32
Colin Archer sailing pilot boat, 8

Comfort, 1, 2
Comfort ratio, 8
Computers, in design, 23, 24, 37, 96
Construction, 81-95
    drawings, 96-97
Convex sections, of hull, 14, 29
Cores, FRP, 92, 94-95
Costs, 1, 2, 18, 50, 60
    design, 102
    engine, 59
    maintenance, 2
    metal hull, 87, 88
    stove fuel, 72
Cowhorn, Block Island, 68
Cruisers, 33, 69
    Arctic Loon, design of, 124-25
    centerboard, 43
    coastal, 2, 118-19
    Deer Isle 28, design of, 108-09
    express, 2
    full-keel, 23
    Morgane Le Fay, design of, 112-13
    Orca, design of, 118-19
    Sandingo, design of, 122-23
Cushions, 70, 77
Cutter, 53, 54
    gaff, 53

D

Daysailers, 1, 2, 15, 42
Deadrise angle, 7, 14, 21, 29
Deck edge, *see* Sheer

Decks
    metal, 88
    plan for, 97
    wood, 85-86
Deer Isle 28, design of, 108-09
Deknatel, John, 63
Design, small-craft, learning, 101
    (*see also* Plans)
Design, selecting, 99-100
Diagonals, 22, 23, 35-37
Dinettes, 72
Dinghy, 15, 16, 102
Displacement, 3, 5, 8, 16
Displacement/length ratio, 7-8
Distress signals, visual, 130-31
Dory, 10
    cruiser, 11

E

Edmonds, Arthur, 20, 58
Electrolysis, 85, 87-88
Engines, 2
    backfire flame control, 129
    diesel, 59
    gasoline, 59
    outboard, 60-61
    stern drive, 60-61
    wing, 60

F

Fairbody line, 21
Fairing, 35, 88, 103
Fastenings, in construction, 85, 87
Fiberglass materials, 89-92
    cloth, 89-90
    E-glass, 90
    Fabmat, 90, 91
    mat, 90, 91
    resin, 90, 92
    S-glass, 90
    woven roving, 90, 91
Fiberglass-reinforced plastic (FRP),
    89-94, 103
Fiddles, 72, 77
Fire extinguishers, 129-30, 132
Fire protection, 80, 129
Fishing boat, outboard, 1

Flam, 29-30
Flare, 29-30
Flotation lines, 3
Foretriangle area, 6-7
Formica, 86
Frames, hull, 24
    chine, 85
    composite, 85
    laminated, 84
    longitudinal, 85
    metal, 87
    sawn, 83-84
    steam-bent, 83, 84
    transverse, 87
Freeboard, 1, 31-32
Fuel fills, 79
Fuel tanks, 80, 132
Furnishings, 77

G

Galley gear, 72-74, 79, 80, 132
Garvey, 10, 68
Gasoline consumption, 2-3
Generators, 58, 133
Gunkholing, 2

H

Handrails, 78
Harness, safety, 78
Harris, Bob, 39
Headsails
    drifters, 51
    flankers, 51
    genoas, 51
    reachers, 51
    spinnakers, 51
    working jibs, 51
Heat exchanger, for hot water, 75
Heel, angle of, 25, 31, 32
Helm, 57
Herreshoff, Nathanael, 38
Horns, 130
Houseboats, 2, 68
Hughes, Kurt, 19, 20
Hulls
    arc-bottom, 11
    asymmetrical, 33

    balanced, 33
    chine-planing, 26, 85
    cold-molded, 83
    convex, 14
    deadrise, 11
    deep-V, 14-15, 27
    displacement, 29, 47, 69
    double-ended, 16
    flat-bottom, 9-10, 21
    garvey, 68
    houseboat, 68
    lapstrake, 81
    metal, 87-89
    monohedron, 7
    multiconic plywood, 86
    planing, 8, 15, 29, 47, 48, 58
    radius-bilge, 18, 87
    related to rig, 56-57
    Rosslyn sharpie, 11, 13
    round-bilge, 15, 86
    round-bottom, 15
    sharpie, 10, 11, 21
    scow, 68
    semi-planing, 29
    U-section, 15
    V-bottom, 11-13, 15, 21, 23, 69
    warped-bottom, 7, 15, 48
    wineglass, 16, 21
    wood, 81-85
    yacht, 13
    Y-section, 16, 21
Hull shapes, 9-20, 63-67, 69
Hunt, Raymond, 14, 63
Hydroplanes, 59

I

Iceboxes, 74
Insulation, of metal boats, 89
IOR (International Offshore Rule),
    26, 31

J

Joiner sections, 98
Joints, fiberglass deck/hull, 93

K

Keels

bilge, 47
centerboard, 40, 43
fin, 38, 40, 69, 97
full, 38, 40-42
lead-ballast, 85
modified full, 38
short, 38
twin, 47
Keel line, 21
Ketch, 53, 54, 55
gaff, 55
wishbone, 53

L

lapstrake, 81
Lapworth, Bill, 38
Lateral plane, 38-48
powerboat, 47-48
Lead, sailboat, 56-57
Leeboards, 43-44, 46
Leecloths, 70
Leeway, 25, 43
Length on Deck, 3
Length Overall (LOA), 3, 33, 63
Life jackets, 78
Lifelines, 78
Lifesaving devices, 130
Life Sling, 79
Lights, navigation, 130
Lines drawing, 21-37, 96
Lloyds, 80
Load Waterline Length (LWL), 3, 6, 7, 21, 23, 25, 26, 30, 33, 62, 63
Lofting, 103
Longest perpendicular (LP), 51

M

Metal, in construction, 29, 68, 87-89, 102
aluminum, 88-89
steel, 88
Midship sections, 9
Mizzen, 54
Modifying a boat, 100
Molds, 24
Moment to Trim (MT1), 3-5
Munroe, Commodore Ralph, 42-43
Motorboat

displacement, 24, 34
high-speed, 12
Multihulls, 18-20
Mylar, advantage of for patterns, 24, 103

N

National Advisory Committee for Aeronautics (NACA), 40
National Fire Protection Association, 80
Newick, Dick, 19
Numbering, Coast Guard–required, 128

O

Offsets, 24, 96

P

Paints, 88, 89
Performance, 1
Periodicals, boating, 135
Perry, Bob, 31, 39, 40
Plans, 96-101
custom or stock? 97, 99
Plan view, 21, 32-34
Plumbing, 74-75
Plywood
for decks, 85-86
for hull construction, 15, 19, 29, 65, 68, 81-87
grades of, 86-87
Pooping, 32
Ports, 79
Pounds per Inch Immersion (PPI), 3
Powerboats, 69
berths, 70
chine-hull, 26
planing, 34, 35
semi-displacement, 15, 34
semi-planing, 34
Powering, 58-61
Prismatic Coefficient (CP), 5, 6, 26, 35
Profile, 21, 96
Propeller
sizes, 58-59
stainless steel, 87

Pulpits, bow, 78
Pumps
bilge, 58, 79, 133
diaphragm, 79
hand, 79
hydraulic, 58
sink, 74

Q

Quarters, aft, shape, 26

R

Racer, 15, 34, 70
America's Cup, 2
IOR, 2
ocean, 2
Ratios, design, 62
Refrigeration compressors, 58, 74
Reverse, steering in, 40
Rig, 49-50
Bermudan, 49-51, 54, 55
gaff, 49, 50, 51, 55
jibheaded, 49
lateen, 49
lugsail, 49
marconi, 49
sliding gunter, 49
types, 51
Rig-hull relationship, 56-57
Royal Ocean Racing Club (RORC), 54-55
Rudder, 40-42
aft-hung, 40
balanced spade, 40
skeg-hung, 40
Rumrunner, 68
Rust, 88

S

Safety, 50, 55, 57, 59, 65-66, 68, 78-80, 128-33
Sail area, 25, 26
Sail area/displacement ratio, 8
Sailboats, 2, 4, 8, 34
multihull, 18-20
powering, 58
racing, 15, 34, 70
rigs, 49-57

Sailing magazine, 99
Sail plan, 97
Scarf joint, 86
Schooners, 12, 51, 53, 54, 59
    Boston pilot, 120
    coastal, 68
    gaff, 53
    Sophia Christina, design of, 120-21
    staysail, 53
    Tree of Life, 51, 55, 85, 126-27
Scows, 9-10, 11, 13, 68
Screws, single or twin, 59-60
Seacocks, 79, 87
Seaworthiness, 1
Sections, 21
Section shapes, 26-29
    aft quarters, 26
    stern, 26
Settee fronts, 43
Sharpie, 10, 21-22, 43, 68
Sheer, 32, 63
Sheerline, 21, 62, 67
Showers, 74-75
Skeg, 34, 40
    twin, 48
Skeg line, *see* Keel line
Skipjack, 68
Sleeping space, 70-72
Sloops, 53, 54
    Friendship, 68
    Maine, 10, 54
    star-class, 38
    Sunshine, design of, 114-15
Sole, 2, 68, 70, 72, 92
Spar drawing, 97
Spars, 49, 50
Specifications, 97
Speed, 2
Speed/length ratio, 6, 8
Splash box, 60

Sports fisherman, 2
Stability
    houseboat, 68
    with beam, 24, 25, 32
Standards and Recommended Practices for Small Craft, 80
Standards, for Courtesy Marine
    decal, 131-32
    equipment, 132-33
Steam launch, 69
Stephens, Olin, 38, 40
Sterns
    canoe, 66
    double-end, 66
    fan tail, 66
    heart-shaped, 66
    lifeboat, 67
    pinched, 26
    pinky, 66
    powerboat, 67
    reverse, 66-67
    rocket ship, 66
    shape of, 26, 66-67
    transom, 66, 67
Storage space, 70, 75
Stoves, 72-74, 80
Straps, safety, 79
Swagman, design of, 110-11

T

Teak, for decks, 86
Teredos, 43
Toerails, 78
Toilets, 74
Topsides, 7, 29-31
Trawler, 69
Trimaran, 19, 20
Tripp, Bill, 40
Tugboats, 69
Tumblehome, 30-31, 63, 67

U

U. S. Power Squadron, 3

V

Ventilation, 75-77
    flying saucer, 77
    natural, 128-29
    powered, 129

W

Water closet, 74
Water, keeping it out, 79
Waterlines, 22
Weather helm, 57
Weatherly, 33, 34
Weekender, 2
Wetted Surface (WS), 5
Whistles, 130, 132
Whitby 42, 21, 23
Windows, cabin, 67, 79
Wood, 81-87, 102 (*see also* Plywood)
    fastenings for, 85
    hull framing with, 83-85
    hull, 86-87
    planking, 81-83

Y

Yachts
    Aragosa 38, design of, 116-18
    catamaran, 20
    cutter, 26
    metal displacement, 18
    motor, 34
    racing, 40
    sailing, 24, 32, 33
    workboat, 16
Yawl, 53, 54